GRIPPY SOCK VACATION

BY:
KARLEE JO MERTENS

GIFT AN AUTHOR PUBLISHING, LLC
DENTON, TEXAS

Contents

Disclaimer

Grippy Sock Vacation is based solely upon my personal experiences after I checked myself into a behavioral unit and my healing journey after that. This is a memoir and not meant to diagnose or give medical advice. If you or someone you love is experiencing mental health symptoms, please seek qualified medical and psychiatric advice.

If you or a loved one is experiencing suicidal ideations or have a plan, please immediately go to the nearest hospital or dial 988, The National Suicide and Crisis Prevention Hotline. They have trained people available 24 hours a day, 7 days a week.

Some details and names have been changed in order to respect the privacy of others who appear in my story.

All of the knowledge and definitions in this book are from memory or pamphlets given out at the hospital to me. This is my story of how I ended up checking myself into a behavioral unit at twenty-three and my experiences throughout this chapter of my life.

THE DRIVE UP

It's quiet. The type of quiet where you can hear each other breathe. I hear the shuddering in between breaths from my two sisters who surround me. I feel nothing. *Numb* would be a great word to describe it.

Tears stream down my face without permission. I'm unsure which tear represents which thought, as they're all entangled in a big, knotted mess in my head. My hazel eyes burn.

It's as if no one is sure what to say in a situation like this. My dad, who'd usually be making some sort of joke, is silent. My mom, who'd usually have some story to tell us, is dissociated. My older sister, who *always* has something to share, is silent with her hand on my leg.

My younger sister, who seems never to cease to have some sarcastic comeback that'd make you giggle, is crying as she lies on my shoulder. Then there's me, the elephant in the room (car) in the middle, numb, dissociated, comatose. I am in the middle of an amazingly supportive family. Yet, I feel nothing close to gratitude. Again, I feel *nothing.*

I mean, I feel some nerves as I enter this hospital, with *American Horror Story Asylum* stuck in my head. I tend to get nervous more often than not when doing new things, as well as meeting new people. Other than some nerves, irritation, and guilt, I feel nothing.

I remember feeling guilty that I was "that child." That my parents and sisters had to not only witness me go through the shit I did but now have to take me to a hospital for the mentally ill. It was a lot to process. I felt guilty for the effort and support they often showed me. It was hard not to feel spoiled, favored, or coddled sometimes. I continuously feel bad about the money involved in all these visits and stays as well. I'm fortunate to even be able to go to a mental hospital, really. What a strange thought?

I've struggled with depression and anxiety for as long as I can remember. Generalized Anxiety started around age fourteen, Clinical Depression around sixteen, and now, being twenty-three, I have been diagnosed with ADHD, insomnia, and bipolar 1 disorder. Quite the resume, right? I've been on the same medications for my depression and anxiety for over five years while being unmedicated for my other issues. I was eager and excited about the medication change. Little did I know how terrible medication changes can be to your physical, mental, and emotional health.

I have a sister who is two years older than me and a sister who is four years younger than me, with yours truly stuck in the middle. We're an extremely close trio. Although, it hasn't been the way we are now our whole lives. At first, with Kenzie and I being two years apart, we were closer, with Lil Nug being too young for most of the things Kenzie and I did. It wasn't until Lil Nug was around twelve that we could talk freely and not have secrets from the youngest. She learned quickly not to tattle. Now, all of us being in our twenties, we are fortunately incredibly close. We've definitely had our fights and still do sometimes like any siblings do.

However, I think they somehow make us closer in the end.

First, we have McKenzie, the optimistic, kind, outspoken, stubborn yet cuddly, being the eldest. She's the one who has a story that isn't actually that interesting at all. Still, somehow, she makes it interesting by her ability to describe any story with her unique excitement. Her playful, Capricorn energy definitely fits her persona. Kenzie is also our emotional rollercoaster. Sometimes, she'll be telling a happy story, and she'll start sobbing happy tears. She has such a tender heart. Bless her amazingly kind soul. I'm very grateful to have had such an amazing sister to look up to all these years.

Next, we have Lindsey, the Little Nug as I affectionately refer to her. The one who consistently makes you laugh. The soft-spoken listener with an insane sense of humor and an I-Don't-Give-A-Crap-What-Others-Think-Of-Me-Attitude. I'll put in concrete that I want to be like my younger sister when I grow up. It's not that Kenzie wasn't someone I would like to be like because she is, but because Lindsey has a way of viewing the world that mesmerizes me. Her persona also fits the outgoing, stubborn, bubbly Scorpio energy too well. She matured beyond her years, encompassing one of the biggest hearts I've encountered.

Lindsey's forever been my listener, the one who knows how to handle me and my episodes. Kenzie loves to hug it out while she cries. This usually makes me feel worse because I don't want to cry or see her cry on behalf of me. I also typically don't want to be touched before or during a breakdown. *Sometimes*, it can be arranged afterward. Physical touch during a breakdown makes me break down even worse. Kenzie gives a different kind of support—her words of wisdom and faith. I love my sisters so much. I'm so grateful for them and all their support throughout the years. It's hard to imagine who and where I'd be without them and their constant care.

I usually don't let my sisters lie on top of me because I become uncomfortable, so I never fall asleep. But surprisingly, this time, it feels okay as they both lie on me. Both of their long brown hair hangs off my shoulders, entangling in my sandy blonde hair. Their blue eyes stream more tears. I eventually ended up in my older sister's lap with my younger sister lying on me. The silence beside the sniffles is too much, too loud. Soon after, my demons started to attack me, so I went to bed.

I nearly went to a unit at age sixteen but manipulated my parents into thinking I was just fine. I'm honestly grateful I went now versus when I was a teenager. My mindset at twenty-three is positive, wanting to learn and take away as much as I can from my stay. Verses when I was sixteen, I was very negative about the whole experience and scared of what others would think. I was also battling a lot of denial about having some of my symptoms and struggles. Now, being more self-aware of the conditions I have makes entering the unit much more doable. Living in a small town, it would be the talk of the town if I ended up being admitted at just sixteen. As an adult, I have a bit more privacy, and that is helpful as I take this step.

Sadly, there is something very intimidating about going to a mental hospital during your middle and high school years. Everyone knows. Everyone talks. You are just trying to focus on taking care of yourself and why you are in the hospital, but the unneeded background noise and drama in your head during your stay is at the forefront of your mind. You want a clear mind to be as optimistic and open as possible. This allows you to strategize a healthy end goal for your mental health. I feel like at sixteen, I would have gone in and participated in nothing, talked to no one, and would have left the unit worse than before I entered it without the maturity that I now have.

Before I closed my eyes, my last thought was wishing our family was heading on a family trip somewhere like when we were younger. I can't remember the last time we were all packed in the vehicle like sardines, but it brings me comfort.

However, the current reality is the whole family is taking me to get dropped off at a behavioral unit.

CHECK-IN

I wake up from my nap, dazed and confused.

For a split second, I forget. All of a sudden, I remember, *we're here.* A surge of anxiety wipes over me as my body turns hot. I choke back my tears as my parents turn around to look at me to see if I'm ready. I sit in between my beautiful sisters and give them both a look of, "all right, let's do this."

We all stumble out of the vehicle, grab my things, and head inside. As soon as we entered the behavioral unit, I felt trapped, claustrophobic even. My two sisters looked a little scared, whether that was for me or of the people in the lobby. There is quite a diverse group in the lobby. An excellent first impression, if you will. (That was sarcasm.)

I didn't know what to expect as I voluntarily checked myself in. I didn't know what to expect at all. I was merely given little tidbits of what to anticipate. I packed pictures and letters from friends and family to help me while I was there. Books, piano sheet music, my journal, and other important items to me that also brought me comfort. Regardless of how or why, I wasn't given any of my items back. They probably thought, "This girl has too much shit, just give back some of her clothes and her tampons." Speaking of my tampons, I hid two nicotine sticks amongst the other tampons, praying the nurses would miss them. Well, they didn't say anything, but when given my tampons, they weren't there. An epic failure. Fricken shit.

On a side note, after getting discharged, I was given back the rest of my items. Within those items, remained my two nicotine sticks wrapped carefully in their wrappers. I joked with the nurse discharging me and asked, "So, would these have been okay if whoever grabbed my tampons grabbed ones with nicotine in them?" The nurse cackled and said, "A man definitely went through your things because any woman would have caught that and made them do a room check on you." I was just like, "Ha, oh… so lucky me, I guess?" It was kind of comical. She just laughed and went, "Just put those back in your bag and be on your way with them," with a wink.

I was given a list of things I could not bring and things I could and followed it… sort of. So, I packed a suitcase full of comfy clothes and multiple items I did not need. Leggings, sweats, hoodies, t-shirts, and sports bras are the main items in the suitcase, besides the other random journals, self-help books, piano music, and letters. I think I even packed a little crochet kit.

That and the fifteen pairs of fuzzy socks I thought I needed. They only gave me seven back when all was said and done. One of the few mistakes I made while packing was only packing one crewneck. I didn't even think about the strings in my hoodies. Frickin A, there are literally so many ways to harm yourself, it's stupid! I didn't know about half of these tactics until entering the hospital. *But strings, come on, Karlee. Strings?! All I want is to hide under my hoodie. I feel so safe in my hoodies. Fuck.*

As the nurses go through my things, I get checked in. We had to leave my sisters behind, and I later got a story of what they experienced in the waiting room. As my parents and I continued further into the hospital, the hallways got longer, the locks got more intense; less windows and more doors. It feels like we are in a maze on our way to some epic discovery. *A discovery of what's wrong with me, maybe?*

We talked to multiple doctors and staff to make sure I 'qualified' to be checked in. As soon as you say you are, have been, or still think you could be suicidal, it's game over—you're checked in. I have been suicidal for months, in secret. Overdosing on pills, drowning in the bath, car accident ideations. I had attempted pills, drowning, drinking, and cutting. It wasn't until I was staring at a gun we owned a little too close and a little too long that I realized I needed to get more help. A week later, and here we were.

I was told to show up comfy, so I was wearing a t-shirt, my boyfriend's hoodie, leggings, and fuzzy socks with Uggs. (Super original, I know.) They instantly snatched my hoodie; I even had the strings taken out and everything, but nope. I'm then led into a private room with the nurses and get a proper pat down. I am monitored by a female nurse while the other male nurse waits at the table while I get undressed. *Talk about uncomfortable.* I make eye contact with the nurse about five times as I awkwardly change into a hospital gown. After getting changed into the gown, I get patted down. After my pat down, I have to squat and cough to make sure I am not smuggling anything down there.

After this "fun little exercise," I'm given my clothes back. I gasped as I got dressed, realizing what t-shirt I was wearing. I honestly think, "Ha, oh well, they didn't say anything," so I proceed to put my shirt back on and giggle. Mom and Dad got invited back into the room. I step out from behind the curtain, and my dad bursts out laughing and goes, "Karlee, your shirt!"

The comical shirt is green with little letters where a pocket would go that says, "Don't fucking touch me." I laugh and look at the nurse with a look that says without speaking, "Is this okay?" He giggles and goes, "Oops, definitely missed that in check-in. Yeah, if you could just change." I get a different t-shirt and proceed. *How funny would that have been as a first impression, though? Just prancing around in a passive-aggressive, vulgar shirt in a mental hospital? No big deal.*

Things got a little more real after they took my clothes and things. I can't recall much of check-in, to be completely honest. I dissociated and went numb for over seventy-five percent of it. I remember being nudged and awakened by them asking for my signature or initials. I'll never be able to unsee the look on my parents' faces during this entire process. They were trying to keep things light, but any time it was idle, everyone's head went to the same place…Where we were. What we were doing. This is what I recall most.

There is one point I can't ever forget during check-in, though. My mom, dad, and I were in a room waiting for the next doctor to come in. This is probably the fourth room we'd been in at this point. The tensions continued to get higher, and my body became tense. I couldn't get my leg to stop shaking. I was so anxious and regretting my decision in some parts of my mind and trying to calm it down in others.

I finally gave in and grabbed my vape out of my bra while looking my parents in the eye, "I'm sorry. I'm really anxious, and this might be my last hit for a week." They both giggle and surprisingly, my mom, who is not fond of my addiction and is not a smoker, goes, "Can I hit it? Damn." Of course, she doesn't actually hit it, but we giggle. Shortly after, the doctors come in. I sigh and hand my vape over to my parents.

The loving hugs given to my parents; I'll never forget. Deep down in my stomach, it was knotted. I fear, somehow, that I will never see them again. More accurately, it is the unknown of *when* I will be able to see them again that nags at me.

The hospital staff gave me a packet they apparently went over with me, and I was taken into the unit. There were so many damn key cards! I keep thinking about escaping before I see how many obstacles I am going to get thrown at me. The nurse who went with me also just stared at me like she knew what I was considering. Her face says, "What are you going to do?" I am not going to run. I understand why I am here, even if I'm nervous. *You checked yourself in because you want to have the will to live. You want to get better. You have a positive outlook this time versus when you were sixteen and manipulated your parents into thinking that you were 'just fine.' Tough it out.*

SISTERS IN THE WAITING ROOM

NOVEMBER 28, 2022

This chapter is a special guest chapter. It will be from my two sisters' point of view. The reason for this is my disassociation during the entire check-in and discharging process. They ended up telling me this story as soon as I got discharged. I was completely overstimulated and disassociated from the world. I didn't comprehend a word. It wasn't until writing this book that I finally heard the story, forgetting about being told already.

Lindsey's story:

The drive went by much faster than I wanted on the way there. I was dreading what we were about to go through. I wrote a note for KJo about when she got there. I did this in hopes that no staff would take it, so she could keep it and have at least one note with her. I really hope that she was able to keep it and read what I had to say to her. Hopefully, she could read through all of my misspellings. It was a hyped-up, emotional note from my big, fat, juicy heart. I also added in a couple of my favorite Bible verses that went along with what she was going through.

When we got there, I didn't know what to expect. I just hoped we would get a proper goodbye while praying Karlee wasn't feeling scared or imprisoned. When we got into the building, we had to check-in. There were a lot of people sitting there, but I remember one person in particular. There was one man who was extremely upset while making a scene because he desperately wanted medication.

When we went to sit down, Karlee and my parents entered the unit, but McKenzie and I had to stay back. I understood, but I was also just confused. I wished we knew what was going on. We sat there for a very long time. Hours. The entire time, there was a native woman with crazy fuzzy pj pants and colorful socks with crocs encompassing them. I remember thinking her hair was nuts and that she looked a tad sleep-deprived. I assumed she got out and was waiting to get picked up. However, literally the whole time McKenzie and I sat there and waited, this woman would not take her eyes off me. She had the most somber, straight face on. I would even catch her, and she wouldn't even react, but she would continue to stare.

There were also a lot of cops there. One moment I'll never forget was seeing a man who was getting escorted by two cops. They walked right in front of McKenzie and I. McKenzie texted me, and our conversation went as follows.

"McKenzie: what the fuck."

"Me: I know right. He looks so unhappy."

"McKenzie: No. He literally had handcuffs."

"Me: Oh. Really???"

"McKenzie: How did you not notice that?"

I don't know how I overlooked that. After that, I looked back over at the woman to see if she noticed, and sure enough, she was still staring straight at me. Unphased. I was so drained, and we sat there for a while, so I ended up closing my eyes for a bit. When I opened them, sure shit, she was still there, still staring. I felt bad for her. I had no clue what she could be going through. I hope she's doing okay. I'm actually thankful that she was making me uncomfy because it took my mind off of what we were there for.

After a while, Karlee and my parents came back. Mckenzie and I were so relieved and excited to see them. I couldn't wait to talk to them about what we were experiencing and also to see how Karlee was doing. Unfortunately, that's not what happened. She had to leave us right away.

We literally could only say "goodbye" and "I love you," and she had to go. It was very rushed, and I was very upset that I hadn't received the proper goodbye that I had been hoping for. Even though I don't know exactly what I was expecting because I literally was going to see her within the week. Still, I was just sad and felt like she was going to be gone forever after she left.

We got into the car and we left. I just remember the car being very emotional, and no one really talked. It was just silent. We all were very happy and proud of Karlee for being brave enough to not take on her demons alone and for her self-awareness. She knew she needed help, which we are all very proud of. However, for some reason, it just hurts so bad that this was still happening.

I know there were a lot more details and things that happened that day, but for some reason, I just can't seem to remember. I think my brain knew that it was so hard on all of us, so I pushed it away. I can't remember even when I try to remember.

I do recall getting back to Watertown to the apartment where both my roommates were. They were so confused and had no idea where I'd been or what was going on. I knew I needed to tell them at some point, but I was so tired and wanted to get my crying out alone. I also didn't want to talk about it, so I just remember laying in bed and going to sleep.

That week was a hard week for all of us. I know it was. I got to call Karlee the next day. I remember it being tough because I could hear in her voice how sad and unhappy she was. I was aware that when I was talking to her, even though it might've made me feel a little bit better to hear her voice, I think it might've been harder for her to hear mine. I knew that she missed us and wanted to be out. Even though she knew that this was a good idea for her. She started crying, and I remember her saying, "Oh no. They saw me crying. I have to go."

I know the people working there are only there to help her and make her feel better. For some odd reason, that still really made me hurt, thinking she was about to get in trouble or something. Although I knew that wasn't the case.

A couple days after Karlee was in the hospital, I was lucky that my schedule allowed me to go see her one night when I got done with school. One day after school, I drove to Sioux Falls to surprise her. She had no clue that I was coming. When I got there, I was a little bit nervous because it was dark out. I was in Sioux Falls alone and had no idea who would be at this type of hospital at this time of night.

When I got there, I remember being in that waiting area to check in, and there were a ton of people there again. A lot of cops were in the room who were not there the first time we went to check in. I was confused.

Soon after, a man came out with chains on his feet and arms, all locked up. I felt bad for him. All I could feel was that this poor man must've done something that he wasn't able to control, and now he's in trouble. I just felt bad.

He came out looking absolutely drained, exhausted, and sad. The cop was really nice to him. I remember their conversation from a distance faintly. It went something like this:

"Cop: How have you been?

How are you doing?

Don't worry about your medication, we have it."

"Man: Where are we going?"

"Cop: We have to go back to jail."

He looked so defeated and sad. I remember thinking, "This poor guy." After they left, I was able to talk to the secretary woman. I told her that I was coming to visit my sister, who was in unit B. She told me what way to go and how to get up there. I remember thinking, "what the heck… how is she expecting me to just find my way around this ginormous hospital by myself? And what if I was a psychopath and would go see people that I wasn't supposed to?"

I remember finding the one elevator she told me to go to, but I think I hit the wrong button or something. I ended up in a place where a man who was working looked at me, and I thought, "I knew

I was not in the right spot." So I was like, "Hey, can you show me how to get to this area?" He first looked at me confused and then went, "Oh yeah, that's not here," and then explained to me where to go. I was so embarrassed but leave it to me to get lost.

Once I finally found my way up to where Karlee was, there was a really nice lady who told me what to do. She told me to put some of my belongings into a locker because they're very strict on what was allowed in the units with these patients. I walked in after all my belongings were put away, and I remember seeing Karlee standing there. The look on her face just made me so happy. She was so shocked and happy to see me.

When I got there, it was time for her to eat supper, which I was kind of excited about because I had never eaten anything yet. I was starving myself, so of course, Karlee was selfless and gave me a couple of the treats on her tray. Karlee introduced me to some other people that she had met and was hanging with while she was there. They were really cool. I was really happy that she wasn't alone and had people around her age who were going through similar experiences. They were all really nice.

Karlee showed me where she was staying and showed me some of the crazy knick-knacks that they have there to make sure people won't hurt themselves. It's crazy… the imagination of it all. Some people have probably tried insane things in the past. Now, they need to suicide-proof the rooms and the facility the way they do.

Karlee and I were talking, and it was really nice that we could see each other. I hoped that she was happy that I was there and felt some comfort and relief. Honestly, I really needed it for myself, too. I stayed 20 minutes longer than I was supposed to. One of the staff members gave us some time alone but then said, "I'm really sorry, but you need to leave". Which I totally understood.

I told Karlee not to worry about all of us and just worry about herself. I also added that we're all OK and very proud of her. Once I left, I'm not gonna lie; I was terrified to walk to my vehicle. I was very tempted to talk to a policeman and ask if they could walk through the parking lot with me because I'm terrified of big cities. On the other hand, I was also thinking to myself, "Lindsey, don't be a baby, you're fine". So I ran to my car instead of asking the policeman.

As soon as I got to my truck I locked the door and got out of there. On my way back to Watertown, I remember already feeling a lot better leaving the hospital this time than I did the first time. I called my parents and my sister to tell them how everything went. I wanted to give them some peace of mind that she was doing well and this was a good place for her to be right then.

I'm extremely thankful that my sister was brave enough to take those steps and go to the hospital. That week was hell for all of us. Still, I would much rather go through that type of thing again. One million times over again versus Karlee trying to fight this battle alone and not getting help.

I remember when Karlee came home from the hospital, and all of us were home together, she decided to read some stuff that she had written in her journal while she was there. While she was reading it, I just remember all of us being so interested in her words.

Personally, I felt like I was there with her. Her words were so strong, and she has such a good way with words.

McKenzie and my mother were the first ones to say it. Still, they told Karlee, "you should definitely write a book, your words are so empowering, and this could really help others." We all agreed and hoped that she would follow through with this, but it was never something we were going to push or pressure her about. That's something that she would need to make her own decision on and do on her own. Once Karlee told us she was writing a book, we were all very proud of her. Not only to help others but also knowing that it was going to be therapeutic for her to write these things down herself again.

I know this experience helped Karlee in so many ways, and I pray that this book of hers gets into the right hands. I hope her words can help others who struggle with mental health as well.

McKenzie's story:

I met my parents and sisters at the Flying J truck stop because that was the easiest meeting location for them coming from home and me, coming from my other home. My basketball season had begun just a week before, and I didn't have a surplus of personal days to take being a newer teacher in the district. Still, my mind was nowhere to be found other than on my sister and with my family.

I remember leaving work early, and one of my students asked me why I was leaving. This question triggered me. I responded with a crack in my throat, "I am going to go see my sister for the afternoon," and this student could sense that I wasn't my happy self. She ran over to me and gave me the biggest hug that I so desperately needed at the time. In a way, this eleven-year-old fifth grader gave me some strength that I didn't know I needed.

I had only told the necessary people why I was leaving early because I couldn't talk about it without feeling weak and crying. And that isn't what I could be right now. Being weak couldn't be an option because, in my head, I needed to give all the remaining strength and love I had to Karlee, my parents, and Little Nug, Linds. I had kept pretty quiet and to myself, but it wasn't hard to pick up on the fact that something had my mind and efforts elsewhere. While I was walking to my car, I remember pausing and standing by my door. I completely lost it, sobbing in the street, right outside of the walls that contained pure happiness and the naivete of children not understanding pain or hurt yet. Ironic.

All I felt was pain. From the moment my beautiful, strong, and smart little sister, my best friend, told me the pain and demons she had been battling consistently for some time now, alone.

How could I not have noticed?

How could my instincts not have kicked in that things weren't okay?

HOW did it come to this point?

Was I really so stuck in my own life that ignoring the people I cherish the most had become easy?

All these emotions and questions ran through my mind day and night, leading up to meeting my family at the Flying J.

I hopped into the car. Karlee Jo was in the middle, Lindsey to her right, and I joined her on the left. Dad was driving, and Mom sat passenger. We had done this exact seating chart before. However, the car was filled with music, movies, or giggles, anticipating the road trip destination we were on our way to.

We were no strangers to passing the time in the car; we spent so much time traveling to basketball tournaments, livestock shows, or anything else to keep us busy when we were kids. Spending countless hours in the car and never running out of things to say or do for hours on end.

But this short fifteen-minute drive from Flying J to the hospital seemed to drag forever, yet not long enough. The entirety of the short drive was spent mostly in silence, filled with sniffles. *Damn it.* I am SO emotional; never have to wonder what I am thinking or feeling. My stupid alligator teardrops are relentless and give away my poker face.

Karlee NEVER lets neither me nor my sister Linds lay on her. She hates being touched or smothered. But she didn't mind having both of us with our heads lying on her lap while she slouched to get comfy. Packed in the backseat like sardines, can't seem to get close enough for us to take away any of her demons that were willing to surrender before releasing her to the hospital.

Pulling up to the hospital, I remember the lump in my throat swelling up like a damn balloon, I could feel the alligator tears roaring to escape the gates of my eyes, but I will not let them. Not now. Now was not the time to show how I was truly feeling on the inside.

I am fully aware of the benefits and needs for Karl's stay at the hospital. Honestly, I think a lot of my emotions are genuine feelings of gratitude that we are driving to a hospital with her to receive help rather than a funeral home for her, too late for help.

Dad did his typical "Alright, I'll drop you all off at the door" gesture, and we all piped back with a "Really, Dad? No. Go park the car". A sweet gesture, really, but not the time. Read the room, Dad. I mean, come on, man. As we piled out of the car, everyone offered to help carry one of the four over-packed bags.

Karlee packed for her stay.

No surprise she so excessively overpacked. That's Karls. Doesn't matter where we are going, what we are doing, or how long we are gonna be gone; Karls packed for a month-long trek across the world. I giggled a little and thought, "Karls? Are you ever planning on coming back or what?!". But Karlee wanted to carry a majority of her things. I guess she was still trying to prove to us that she really wants this and that she's ready for help. Walking into the building in typical Mertens fashion, we go to the wrong door.

After finding the correct entry way, we made our way to the check-in desk. *Dang, this place has just about as much security as a damn airport.* Linds and I made our way to the comfy seats while Mom, Dad, and Karl went to the counter. I remember watching Karl as she told the front desk lady her name and that she was here for check-in. Her voice was always faint and meek, but today, it was different because this short sentence held a lot of power, and she sounded so bold in her words, confident yet unsure.

She grabbed the paperwork and clipboard. She came back, sat by me, and started filling out the forms. I couldn't help but notice her hands were sweating. The tops of her fingers even glistened. She even looked at me and said, "God damn it, my hands are so sweaty right now." I could tell she was nervous but didn't want to show it. Her sweat glands gave it away as I watched her try to stoically fill out the forms.

Watching the individuals in the check-in area was a lot to stomach. The room was tiny, so small it was like you could hear everyone's thoughts and feel their stares. I also remember the guy who was making an ever-loving scene about how he "Was going to hurt himself," "No one will listen to him," and "I need meds, and I need help."

It was hard not to stare, but my heart hurt for him, and I really couldn't believe my eyes, as I had never experienced anything like this before. Shortly after this, we were pulled from this small gathering space and taken about twenty-five feet down the hall to another much larger waiting room. We found a spot to get comfy, and more waiting continued.

We sat there together as a family, waiting for the next nurse to pull us all to another destination.

While we waited, we all just watched. Occasionally, we made eye contact, raised eyebrows, or shrugged our shoulders. A nurse came and asked for Karlee, and all of us stood up. He looked at us all, waiting for the real Karlee to make herself known. She did, and the nurse asked for her to come back with her parents.

Karlee looked at this man, and this was truly one of the first times I saw Karlee's eyes scared. She asked, "Can my sisters come with too?" and his eyes flashed from Linds and me to Karlee and back to my parents, and he replied with, "No. I'm sorry".

Linds and I assured Karlee it was fine, and we'd be fine, but she didn't believe us. She apologized with her eyes and then disappeared through the heavy hospital doors. Linds and I stood there for a moment longer, looked back at one another, and then found our seats and got comfy.

Little did we know how comfy we actually could have gotten. Shit, this wait was ridiculous. *What could they possibly be doing back there?* We sat and waited and sat and waited and sat and waited some more. People came and went as we remained still in the same seats. I'm fairly certain that our butt prints are still embedded in those seats.

There were times when a nurse would wander through the doors, and we would perk up a bit, hoping Karls would be following, but that didn't happen. One time, when I was sure both of us were about to fall asleep, here came a man with a policeman escorting him on both sides, hands handcuffed. Feet chained together, walking right through the waiting room.

I locked eyes with my sister, and part of me was anxious about the thought of my other sister literally in the process of checking in, being in the same building as an individual who clearly wasn't trusted and needed all the extra security precautions. My heart hurt, and my thoughts consumed my brain as I observed the individuals checking in, walking through, checking out. The family members who didn't make the cut into the back rooms were left out here with my sister and me.

At this point, I am confident that hours had passed since we'd been sitting there, memorizing the patterns on the wall when, all at once, the swinging doors opened, and the familiar faces came shuffling through the doors, looking just the same as when they entered. I felt happy seeing Karl and wanted to fill her in on all the things we had been watching, but that wasn't the case.

The nurse told her to grab her things. Karlee asked if we could come with her to her Unit, but that wasn't allowed. All in a glimpse, Karlee gave both of us a huge hug - mind you, she's not a hugger, said I love you and talk soon and vanished behind the doors. Linds and I stood there in silence, left behind again.

Neither of us could control the immense feelings we felt along with the lumps in our throats. Trying to choke them down was no longer an option. I sat back down in my seat, and Linds sat right next to me for a moment. Then, she laid her head on my lap. Neither of us talked nor looked at our phones; we just sat there, and the teardrops rolled down our cheeks.

My sisters and I are incredibly close. We've not always have we been like this. But as we grew up and the cruelty of the world happened, we began to understand that having two built-in best friends who, no matter what will always have your back was a pretty special thing to cherish. We have matching tattoos, something to remember that no matter what any of us are going through and no matter where we are, our bond and love cannot be broken. When one of us needs additional strength, the two of us step up.

At this moment, my "baby" sister laying in my lap, and the third piece of our trio being checked in to receive more strength and help, I felt weak. I looked down at our matching tattoo, and my eyes glazed over with tears, looking at that middle bird that represents our sweet Karlee Jo.

A short moment later, my parents came into the waiting room, but there was no Karlee or nurse. I remember seeing the pain in both of their eyes. No one said a word. We just all understood that it was time for us to leave, so we walked out the front doors and found our way back to the car. We found a place to eat close by, Qdoba, which is a family favorite.

There is something about the saying, "You never truly know what someone is going through." At that moment, that was all that was rolling through my mind. Was there another family in this restaurant struggling to keep it together because they also dropped someone they love dearly off at a hospital to get more help?

There were many positives and high hopes for this experience for Karlee. I called her every day, thinking back it was probably more for me than it was for her. Truthfully, I talked to her more that week than I usually would because she is awful at responding to text messages and answering her phone.

Our talks were like a roller coaster - one call was good, and the other was bad, and it was basically like that the entire stay at the hospital. I remember calling and asking Karlee how she was doing, and every time, she answered so casually, like, "Yeah, I'm good. Nothing new here, just chilling in my grippy socks and sweatpants and talking to my new 'friends' about what medication change was going to happen next."

When it was time for Karlee to be discharged, I made plans to be home when she got there. *No way I wanted to miss her coming home and telling us all about her found information.* Also, I didn't want her to have to retell her stay more than once because I wasn't sure what the experience was like for her. We gathered in our parents' living room, all five of us home, which is a rare occurrence other than on holidays or special occasions. I suppose this is a special occasion, though, '*Seeking Help Instead Of The Alternative*' reunion back home.

I was so excited to see her and give her a hug, but she was very distant, which isn't abnormal. I thought that she would have been a bit more excited to see us?! Karl started off by saying, "In the hospital, it was always very quiet, and the lights were dim, so all the noise and lights for me right now is a lot. Please lower your voices. Kenzie, I'm talking to you." With that, she began to read her journal, cover to cover, from her stay.

There are a lot of moments in my life where I have felt an abundance of pride for my little sisters, but this is a moment that I truly don't have words to explain my feelings and emotions. I remember thinking how she could really help people with her story and words. The words she wrote and the way she writes are powerful. The journal she read, which is a combination of exercises she did and things she learned, is what you are reading today, Grippy Sock Vacation.

The pride that I felt in that moment in our parents' living room is unmatched by the way I am feeling for her now. Searching for help, publishing HER story, and giving her strength, wisdom, and support to people who need it most.

THE NIGHT OF CHECK-IN

Well, I'm checked in at the behavioral mental health unit. It's less than I expected. I literally feel like I'm in a movie. My counselor had told me I could play the piano, I wouldn't have a roommate, and that there probably wouldn't be anyone here who would make me feel crazier than I already do.

Well…there's no piano, I have a roommate, they took all my things, including my letters from friends and family, and my sad attempt at smuggling in my nicotine vapes in tampon wrappers failed. The last thing I wanted was feelings of withdrawal and constant thoughts of nicotine, but I guess this is how the stay is going to go.

Oh, yeah, there are also a lot of people here who make me feel crazier than I already do. This one lady with schizophrenia keeps screaming at me, "Do you fucking know who I am? I am Winona!" All I could force out of my mouth was a timid, "Cool, I'm Karlee." She repeatedly screamed the same sentence over and over at me until a nurse drug my shocked body away. The nurse proceeded to tell me about her condition and told me to stay clear of that particular patient. *Okay. Got it.*

Soon after, I get a tunnel vision view of what some of the nurses have to deal with daily. A woman is earnestly screaming for her nurse, pushing her red button, demanding to be changed and bathed as she had another accident. God bless nurses! After pulling myself out of shock, I make my way to my room. I had seen enough of the living space for the five minutes that I was out there and needed quiet and safety.

There are three units in the adult behavioral unit. Unit A is the 'worst' unit with the more violent patients. The furniture is literally screwed into the floor, so patients can't throw anything. Unit B, where I am, is a mixed unit that is constantly overflowing with young and old adults alike, with a mixed buffet of issues. Our furniture isn't screwed to the floor but is just extremely heavy. Unit C sounds like a unit for the more comatose drug addicts out of rehab, etc., from what I hear, at least.

Like clockwork, Unit B is continuously filing patients in and out. That's why the curriculum and 'goals' they have set for you are so essential to complete. As well as participation. If you don't participate and sleep away your stay, you're discharged. Suppose you complete the 'curriculum' in a matter of a certain number of days. In that case, you're discharged, even if you feel you aren't entirely ready. They have to keep rotating patients in and out and keep filling the beds as they are highly needed.

In hindsight, I am baffled at how few men are here in this unit. Just to help you conjure up a mental image since we're in an adult unit, the youngest you can be is eighteen or nineteen. The youngest person I met was nineteen. I'd say the unit consists of eighty-five percent of those in their high teens, young and older women, while the other fifteen percent contain men. This is one of the first things I noticed. It pisses me off inside. I ended up having many conversations with the few men here, and all of them answered similarly as to why it took so long for them to finally check themselves in.

I know it's because of how society makes it seem like males shouldn't or can't have mental illnesses. How it is looked at as such a touchy, odd thing for males because they're perceived as "weak" for having this and that they're supposed to be "strong and the leader."

I just think, as a woman, mental health is just assumed to be more of a "normal" thing because we appear "more empathic, sensitive, and caring" to society. Whereas God forbid a man has an illness! Statistics show overwhelmingly that seventy-five percent of suicides are men, with women being the other twenty-five percent. Men are three times more likely to die due to suicide than anyone else. It's honestly somberly comical how reversed that comparison is when you really step back and look at the big picture.

We are all human. We all have the most essential organ—our brain. We both have the left and right sides of the brain. It's not like men have a different anatomy of the brain. Why is it such a crazy thought that men, too, could have mental health issues? Why do you think not many men who commit suicide leave a note, rarely leave an inkling to their family or friends that they had issues going on? Why do you think they hide and suppress their struggles so much harder than us women?

It's not fair. It's complete and total bullshit the way society and social media make it seem so unreal for men to have the same issues women have. I wish more men felt comfortable enough to share what is going on in their heads. I wish this stigma didn't exist for anyone with depression, but I wholeheartedly wish this stigma wasn't heightened for men.

If you are a man reading this and have some sort of mental illness, please talk to someone and seek out help. I think a lot of men feel the women in their lives will think they're unworthy of love or incapable of being a wonderful partner if they have anxiety, depression, or other mental health struggles.

For what it is worth, I think it's courageous and attractive when a man tells me upfront, "Hey, I deal with this, just so you know," versus them going through something and me thinking it's about me when really, they're battling their own demons. We just have no idea about what another person is going through, what eats them alive in their minds. I respect men who are able to be vulnerable and open with family, friends, and partners. I encourage everyone with these issues to do the same. Be open and honest about yourself.

Vulnerability is incredibly beautiful. I wish every soul knew that.

I'm led to my room. My roommate's name is Sandy. She seems just as enthused as I am with having a roommate. I greet her but don't get a response. Sandy has a bigger, shorter build with darker skin than mine, and I'm unsure of her ethnicity. She has brown hair, but half of it was dyed green. Her eyes are brown with deep bags under them. She looks like she's been hit by a truck, twice. I don't know her story, and it seems I never will since, apparently, we aren't communicating.

My room and the entire facility are obviously blander than shit. Grey and white walls everywhere. In my room, there are two beds, two side tables, two shelves, one desk, one chair, a sink, a toilet, a shower, one garbage can, and a Bible. That is it. We do have a window but it's the kind you can't see clearly through. That window seems like an unkind tease to the outside world. The bed is also an inch of fake fluff, stiffer than shit. You can tell they need to have a boatload of 'beds' because whatever this fluff is, it is nothing close to a mattress.

The main living space has minimal things as well. There is a TV showing Harry Potter right now. We get two hours of TV time almost every night. A cute old man in a wheelchair, I'll call Ron, is always hyped up about Harry Potter time. Every night there was a Harry Potter film on. Ron skirts over in his chair and cackles. His face is aglow while watching the movie.

Ron loves to correct whoever gets the character's names or parts wrong. It is all lighthearted corrections, so in return, we all have determined to have fun quizzing him equally. He knows the series down pact. I finally learned how Harry Potter ends while in the hospital, as I have never watched the last two films yet. It's totally on me for not having taken the opportunity to have watched them all before. (Don't hate me, Harry Potter fans.)

There is some exercise equipment, puzzles, games, and tables and chairs everywhere as if we will all get together and make friends. The rooms of the patients line the walls of the living space. My room is around the corner, more towards where the elevators are and where the entrance to get into the unit is. There is a kitchen near the nurse's station that is right around the corner from my room. There are probably five other rooms on the floor for meetings and classes.

We do have a laundry station we can use. I took advantage of this after I had to keep wearing the same shirt and sweatshirt. Then there are the two payphones for the two ten-minute calls we get each day unless someone calls you first.

The pill station is literally out of a movie. A locked mini concession stand type drawing door that is unlocked and locked around the clock. This is right next to the nurse's station. Ever seen *Girl Interrupted,* the one that stars Winona Ryder and Angelina Jolie? Well, watch it. It's a phenomenal film, and this is what I thought of every day when I saw the pill station.

We wait in line for our little cups to be filled with pills and have to take them in front of the nurses right then and there, exactly like in the movie. I choke multiple times because I always have so many damn pills to take and feel pressured being watched to make sure I swallow them entirely. We proceed to show our tongues or smile like, "He, he, all done," and we get a nod before your ears hurt hearing them scream, "Next!"

Then, there is of course, the round table encased with staff that we need to bother all the time. I even had to ask them to unlock my door every time I needed to use the bathroom. This is exceedingly annoying in the mornings.

Later on, throughout my stay, I nearly peed myself a couple mornings. I'd aimlessly stumble around in the dark, not remembering the surroundings of our minimalistic room. I stubbed my toes a few times while cursing, of course.

There is a little locked shelf next to where we get our pills that is filled with other "more dangerous" items like sound machines, radios, pens, fidget spinners, and things like that. We needed to ask the staff to use these items as if the items were lethal. In extreme cases, yeah, they are lethal. It just made me giggle thinking about asking for permission to use a pen like I was in grade school again.

There are probably around ten-fifteen people in the main space when I arrive at the unit around 4:30 p.m. At first, I felt so confused about what everyone was doing at the tables. Then, I realize they are all doing crosswords or coloring. Later, I would really get into drawing and coloring in my spare time. This is such a simple task that really soothes the mind, at least for me.

I came into this place thinking making friends was a possibility. I think there are four "sane" people here. At least from the little I've seen of the other patients so far. It's scary. This place is kind of intimidating. Most people here aren't exactly prancing around in joy. Nearly everyone looks like they hate their life. Most look like they want to die… Well, yeah, I guess we're in the right place, after all.

Everyone looks at me like, why the eff is she here? My profile doesn't match anyone here. I stick out like a sore thumb. The workers, other patients, and I all see it. It makes me feel dumb, being clean, pretty, and 'put together,' I guess.

They freaking took my makeup remover towelettes…. Why? I guess we'll be all natural here. Fine by me. I'm not a big makeup gal. I usually only put on a 'full face' if I'm going to some sort of occasion or if I simply feel like it that day. I'm not that bothered by them taking my makeup and makeup remover, honestly. I guess I thought putting on makeup would be something normal and routine from home to do at the hospital, but I'm learning a new routine here.

I'm craving nicotine like a mother fucker. I wish I could go bang out my emotions on a piano. I *really* was looking forward to that. I forced myself to eat half a cheeseburger with some soggy fries about ten minutes ago. *Go me because I was not hungry!* Patients eat at set times: 7:30 a.m., 12:00 p.m., and 5:00 p.m. I legitimately eat supper between 9:00 and 10:00 p.m. when I'm at home sometimes. This is an adjustment, for sure.

I force myself out of my room and end up isolated by the window. I hear giggles and wish I was sitting by whoever that is. It seems like the group all know each other and have bonded. In a weird, clingy way, I feel left out. *Maybe after group counseling tomorrow, it'll be easier?*

I received my first dose of nicotine gum from my nurse. *What the bloody hell, this shit burns my throat?* I need a rip of my vape. I wonder if they threw away the two new vapes I hid in tampon wrappers? *See, still thinking about nicotine.* The one thing I was so worried about the most was nicotine withdrawal and not having any access to it. I need my mind to relax and focus on my brain and why I'm here.

My roommate has been in our room the whole time I've been out here. That scares me slightly. I want to talk to her, but I've seen that look of dissociation, that fogged-out, blank stare. I had it an hour ago… So, I'll let her be.

I wish I had a single room, piano, nicotine, and a more welcoming reception from everyone. Despite that, we're still going to try and get the best out of this. I hope these things don't stray me too much from why I'm here. I've come into this experience with a positive mindset. Now, hitting reality here, that's not going to be as easy as I thought.

Also, this three-inch pencil can kiss my ass. *Ouch.* Even though the pencils are smaller, they aren't less of a sharp object. I can't understand why they can't give us standard-sized pencils? It's still a pencil, even though it's tiny.

How do I sleep next to a stranger who is struggling like me, if not worse? I'm honestly scared. I want to spend my time with the workers; they make me feel normal. I took a pregnancy test, and honestly, I'm kind of nervous. So that's another fun worry right now. (It turned out it was negative.) These thoughts and more keep plaguing my brain.

I have to pee, so I have to go back to our room for a bit. Maybe I'll talk to her. I honestly want to bawl my eyes out in peace without an audience. I want to be in peace, and so does my roommate. I can tell. As I hold in my pee and injure my kidneys, I start to look out the window. Dissociating, remembering what fresh air and freedom felt like.

Out of nowhere, this older gal with a raspy voice nearly yells, "I'm hot as shit, but I'm going through menopause…what I'd do to be twenty-five again but know what I know now!" That phrase instantly made me feel better and come back to reality. This lady's raspy cackle gives me a sense of joy, too. It reminds me of all my favorite people's laughs.

Especially my best friend's (Happy 24th, Baby Girl.)

Somebody's sigh sounded like Padre after he stands up or takes his shoes off. I hold back tears, suddenly missing him and my family down deep to my bones. Now, I utterly wish I was home. I'm all over the place. Okay, now, I'm going to go pee and maybe talk to Sandy.

All right, so she was sleeping. She snores really bad, unfortunately. Like Padre level bad. My dad needs to use a sleep apnea machine every night now, but before he got this machine, he could rumble the entire house. Hotel stays continually were a treat. Throwing the pillows across the room at him, screaming, "Dad! Shut up!" Back in the present, all I can think about now is how in the 'flippidy floppidy fuck' do I sleep without weed, nicotine, my own bed, and now a bear two feet away?

The staff has been great, so sweet and amazing. This gum has worn off completely, but I feel like a feen asking for more. I also lost my nurse somewhere, and I would need her to get more. So… no go on the gum. I'll have to manage somehow.

Some people here walk around like it is home. Not only that, but it is as if they *love* their home here. Some scramble out of their rooms, excited to continue on with the same curriculum, their daily routine of classes, talks, and 'the schedule.' Others mope around like zombies. I hope I get some sort of comfort soon. Some patients make it look like this *is* their home despite everything. I know that's not the case for me. This is my temporary home.

I wanted to hide in my room all night and write, but the snoring forced me out into the group space.

Which may be a good thing. Maybe someone will talk to me, or I'll get the guts to join the 'normal giggly table.' I feel like the new girl who invaded everyone's space. It's like I'm too put together or intimidating to talk to.

It didn't help that because I voluntarily checked myself in; I was in my street clothes. Most patients were wearing gowns, sweats, sweatshirts, and other clothing provided by staff. I ended up using a sweatshirt of theirs as I only had my one crewneck at one point. It felt as if people instantly judged me for being in my 'normal' clothes. I now know that was just my head.

So... me, myself and I... What brought us here?

Why are we in a mental institution right now? Well, let's go back. I've been trying to pinpoint the exact time this all started, but I think this is something I've surpassed year after year. Now being an adult, with a full-time job, real actual issues being thrown at me and those I love getting older, all combined and brought me here. Let's not forget how I never truly had a 'self-love and self-care' time. I continued to rely on my partners, family, friends, vacations, events, and happy occasions to keep myself happy, which was dangerously unrealistic.

Then, there was tragically losing Annie at the end of August, being faced with the death of someone my age, taken too soon. A human who deserved longer, someone who lived their life to the absolute fullest, every second of every day. *Gone.* She lived one hundred years in those twenty-four years. She lived life like you should. I know they say those who live like that and treat people the way she did get called home sooner to help God. Yet, it's so hard for me to compartmentalize and understand.

There are things I learned today that really stood out. For example, I learned that Dr. Aaron Beck researched depressed patients in the 1960s, came up with a cognitive theory of depression, and later developed Cognitive Behavioral Therapy (CBT). One of the common thinking distortions I learnt about today was *All or*

Nothing Thinking. This is when you view something as either/or without considering the full spectrum and range of possible evaluations. All or Nothing thinkers see things as all black or all white, but never gray. I realized I tend to think this way often, too.

An example of this is sometimes how any of us can think, "If I do not do something perfect, then I am a complete failure," or "If my significant other breaks up with me, I will never find another person." A final example of All or Nothing thinking is, "Because I didn't win an award at work, I am a bad employee."

The second type of common thinking distortion I learned about was *Mental Filtering.* Mental Filtering is when you focus on the negative aspects of a situation and ignore the positive ones. Mental Filtering fails to take into consideration the whole of a person's experience, which often includes things that are both positive and negative. A way to think of it is as a thought like, "My boss gave me positive feedback on my yearly review, but one negative comment, and all I can think about is the one comment that was negative."

We worked on our Goal Sheet today as well, a list of three main categories the psychiatrists specifically picked for my stay for me to work on.

Everyone had different goal sheets. The first subject I chose to work on was the first one that was on my sheet, the absence of self-harm. Later on, I was taught about different types of coping mechanisms and how to turn your negative coping mechanisms into positive ones. (See pages 131-135 for a list of 99 positive coping skills I was given at the hospital.)

xoxo- from KayJo in psych unit B

First Full Day

November 29, 2022

It's 12:15 p.m., and they're going to call me for lunch soon. Last night, I forced myself to go to a couple group sessions. Including the gym, where I played Four Square and made some acquaintances I now call friends; those I can join the table with—Ginny, Sam, Dylan, and Shayla are their names.

Ginny was the cutest little thing. Her energy was so bright and inviting. She's nineteen, short in stature, with bright red hair, the brightest blue eyes, and a turned-up, tiny nose. She has freckles filling her porcelain round face. Freckles encompassed her whole body. (You know, ginger things.) She also had the cutest little heart-shaped lips which are consistently gabbing fun facts and information. She is lost in her life and finds herself here. This isn't her first time here. Her mom is on unit A, the "worst" unit, with Multiple Personality Disorder (MPD), Bipolar Disorder, and early-onset Dementia. This place is kind of Ginny's second home. As she says, "Might as well just stay upstairs when I visit mom every day anyway." She says this with an innocent giggle to follow her dark humor.

Sam is twenty-nine, with brown hair and bright blue bug eyes with a tall build. He had a lisp that made everything he said that much more interesting somehow. Kind of how people with raspy voices catch your ear? He has a great sense of humor and optimism that makes the table feel a little better. He is in here for cocaine, heroin, alcohol, and nicotine addiction. His addiction nearly drove him to kill himself. His friends, being concerned, called the cops, and asked for him to be checked in voluntarily. He did just that.

Dylan seemed to be around my dad's age, late fifties or so. His wrinkles, glasses, words of wisdom, and mannerisms give me that inkling. Every time, he is the one at the table who you think isn't listening, but soon after, he cracks out a dad joke to make us all laugh. He's playful as well, and he plays Four Square and all the games with the 'kids' of the adult unit. He is in here as he's lost and depressed with his life. He's never taken action for his mental health before now. Before having a divorce to deal with, as well as losing his job, he checked himself in to get help for the first time. He feels like my father figure in here.

Shayla's pale with beautiful long black hair and brown eyes. She's tall, around 5'10, with a medium build but timid portrayal of a beautiful self. She is around my age. She has an insane amount of anxiety. I feel so bad for her. I have anxiety, but nowhere near as much as she does. It's funny; she speaks of how hard it is for her to talk in front of others when she's so smart and articulate with her words. Anxiety is something, all right. It makes you doubt yourself when your self shouldn't be doubted at all.

I got in the giggly table, and they've been amazing. A bit bittersweet but sweet bubbly Sam got discharged earlier at 1:00 p.m. today. Without a doubt, I'm so proud and happy for him. I can't help but worry about him and those who get discharged, though.

Last night was probably the worst night's sleep I've had in years. It took me an eternity to fall asleep. I couldn't shut my mind off.

Also, the snoring—*good God.* I had ear plugs shoved in my ears as far as they could go and a sound machine on the nightstand.

Somehow, I still woke up every hour. I was so restless.

I had the weirdest dream about a past boy I'd been with in my sister's room, and I shoved him against the wall questioning the eff out of him. Suddenly, I woke up after my sister and I were throwing fists in her closet. Odd, weird, sobering dream. I remember hearing that people who suddenly stop smoking tend to have weird dreams. Maybe that's the reason?

Next, I wake up to two nurses taking my vitals.

What a way to start your day. The first thing you see through your foggy, tired eyes is a nurse talking to you. She asks you what you want for lunch, telling you to open your mouth for a thermometer and to give them your arm, all whilst being half asleep, dazed and confused. After this routine, day two starts.

I've attended three group sessions today as well as four individual sessions. I'm attending everything and trying to get the most out of every session. I absolutely don't want to hurt anyone. Sometimes, that's where and when my mind travels to suicide and not dealing with any of this at all. But that's a cop-out and would only hurt more people.

Sometimes, I travel to suicidal ideation more than I'd like to admit. I have a hard time wrapping my head around the world and how it works. I have doubts about this life, the point of it all. My purpose in the bigger picture of life. I'm sure others do this, too, but my mind takes it too far. My damn head usually tells me the world is better off without me trying to figure any of those questions out.

Constantly reminding me that I love everyone in my life more than they love me, and that's just how it'll be. That's the position God chose for me.

In other cases, there are times when I'm overly optimistic and carefree about how the world works and why things and people are the way they are. There's this laid-back, chill persona in me that tells me everything actually doesn't matter. You're merely a little speck on a big planet in a galaxy surrounded by other galaxies. You don't matter in the grand scheme of things. I'm aware it sounds blunt and rough, but it helps me to think like this occasionally.

Of course, there's the angel in me that's persistently screaming at me too. The one telling me to lean on my faith. The one telling me everything will work itself out; that everything happens for a reason.

The one reminding me that the whole world *does not* revolve around you and your emotions. Other people have their own lives and their own issues; not everything is about you or even pertains to you.

Do I choose to be alone and heartbroken or stay heartbroken? Either way, I'm heartbroken. I'm so lost. I truly love my partner, but this love for myself is not even half-full. Even three/fourths full would be acceptable. And what about my baby girl, Nali May?

Her parents, who raised her are totally not a thing in her life anymore? I know she's a dog, but none of this seems fair to anyone involved.

I've never been with someone who I've loved so much. That everyone loves so much. He's my mom and dad's son at this point.

I wish I could have figured out my self-love and self-care before I met such an angel.

He says he'll wait for me, "but not years" because he doesn't know "anyone who'd do that." Well, wouldn't you wait however long it takes if you love that person? I told him not to wait, and he said, "What else would I be doing?" I don't know what to do on a multitude of levels.

I honestly cannot imagine my life without him, but I also cannot imagine a life with myself on this level of self-love. He deserves the best version of me, and she isn't here. He thinks he's seen the best version and still loves that version. How do I make sense of this to him, to myself, or to anyone?

8 HOURS LATER

So, while I was journaling, some crazy shit went down. My roommate was sleeping in our room, so I was out in the main space. It was only me and one other girl who got checked in this morning, along with George roaming around aimlessly. "George," a handsome, short but strong, dark-haired man with glasses I've only seen at meal times–exploded!

I'm not sure how long he's been here but he was told he was getting discharged today. The reason was that he did not participate in individual and group sessions or any sessions at all. This was because he was lying in bed all day, sleeping, only coming out to eat.

I get that. I've been there. My roommate is in that phase of sleeping away your thoughts and only getting up to eat. Surprisingly, Sandy has been to a couple sessions today. I'm proud of her. I've been in that phase; I was in that phase. However, I am lucky enough to have a support system, a job, and those who helped me get out of that funk, etc. *I get it.* Still, the way this program works is to put as much into it as you expect to get out of it.

So, I'm sitting there journaling as they tell him he's being discharged, and I finally heard him speak. He screamed, "So, just because I've been the most depressed as I've ever been, sleeping and not 'playing games' or going to all these groups… I'm discharged? I have nowhere to go. I'd be going back to the homeless shelter where I've had guns pulled on me constantly.

I've never committed a crime. I've never assaulted anyone. I did "a drug" once and lost everything. My job, my home, my will to live, everything. I'm begging you to help me! Please help me!"

The screaming at the entire staff, combined with his stomping his feet and hitting his head with his fists, was difficult to hear and witness. He continued to plead, "Aren't you guys professionals? Isn't this what I'm here for? *Help?* And you're sending me back to the shelter where I am terrified of my life? You want me to get killed? You don't think I'm going to try again to kill myself and succeed this time? Please help me! I've never been so scared in my life to go back there and not know if I'll live either due to others or myself." He goes on to plead yet again, "I want treatment. Please." To be honest, there were a lot of "F-Bombs" in there as well. The staff asked who they could call, what they could do, and what he wanted them to do, but George just continued to challenge them by saying that he wanted help, begging and sharing that he had no one. He had no one to call, nowhere safe to go. "Please do not discharge me. I'll do better."

This continued for a good forty minutes. His room was right behind where I was sitting, and he continued to scream at the staff from there while rearranging his room as much as he could. He also tried lifting the heavy ass chairs to throw them. He hardly got them off the ground.

I was honestly kind of scared. Scared of some chair or other item ramming me in the back of the head. The cops came up to escort him. He begged them to let him call "The Link" before he went so he had somewhere safe to go.

I am not sure what 'The Link' is, but I assumed it was some sort of shelter. The staff agreed. As I went to my 4 o'clock class, I saw him on the phone and was escorted out. The staff emphasized that this is a treatment center. "You need to at least try to get involved in the treatment; we cannot provide you a home."

Forced to listen to this conundrum, I can't help but cry for him. I can't stop. I've stated before that if it wasn't for my support system, I'm not sure I'd still be here. Listening to him beg for help, cry about having no one, trembling in fear, scared to enter back into the real world, clearly not better, clawed at my heart.

I feel awful. His words, "You wonder why some people want to commit? Situations like this… you guys are who's supposed to help me, please," continues to keep echoing through my mind.

I get that he needs to put more into this center, but I also have a hard time with how they still discharged him in the state he was in. I hope he got a hold of "The Link," whatever that is. I don't understand why they didn't move him to a different unit or work with him more. He needed and *needs* more help.

I can't stop thinking about him. If he's safe, okay, or alive. Having the support system that I do makes me feel awful, grateful, and blessed. I cannot imagine his plight. I've forever been aware of and grateful for the system I have. Still, that situation actually slapped me in the face.

Every time I've been right there, nearly about to be done with this earth, my support system is who comes to mind. They're the ones who keep me here.

That's another thing I want to rearrange in my head. I want to stay here not only for them but for myself, too.

I think that's why a lot of people tell those with depression and Bipolar Disorder that they're strong… because they truly don't want to be here most of the time. A lot of people with these conditions are still here only for their loved one's sake. Sometimes, my mind wanders to the future when my support system isn't as big as my loved ones pass with time. It worries me.

That's another main reason I came here. As my loved ones get older, too, I have to be able to cope and deal with the loss and death that's inevitable to come. I can't look into the future and know I won't be okay. I want to be able to optimistically look into the future and know I'll be able to get by. I might not be "okay," but at least okay enough to remain fighting on this earth for not only the ones I love but myself as well.

After things calmed down, the new girl behind me a couple tables arrived. Alone, also forced to listen to this conundrum. I decided to join her. It felt like some out-of-body experience, and all of a sudden, I joined a stranger at their table. It felt like we both could use another person after hearing and witnessing all of that. We clicked instantly. She told me her story, and I told her mine. We had small talk until the four o'clock session, which I encouraged her to go to with me.

Her name is Hannah, from Iowa, four hours away. She's from Mexico, with beautiful olive skin and bold brown eyes with dark lashes encasing them. She's a bit taller than I am at 5'7, so I'd guess she's around 5 '9. I got the inkling she was strong, both physically and mentally. She has a beautiful glowing smile with a cute little gap in between her canine and the first premolar on her right side. She has a great sense of humor and one of those giggles that makes you smile. Her love for *Bad Bunny* is something else, I must add, as it seemed like a personality trait for the love bug.

She overdosed on pills last night and was taken to the ER. She got her stomach pumped and was told she *would* be coming to a behavioral unit voluntarily or involuntarily. Involuntarily is when the police need to intervene with cuffs and an escort. She volunteered to come in. She smoked like I did, and we bonded over that, amongst many other things. We had similar relationship situations going on as well.

That's the thing about being here. There's no judgment, and everyone understands depression and anxiety. Everyone understands, no matter what mental health issue you have. There's no need to explain.

There are no looks of pity or judgment.

Ever since Hannah and I got together, we've been sitting by one another. I introduced her to the people and friends who I've been with. Of course, she fits right in. We goofed off together at the gym in Four Square and made each other shine a little. Her giggle grows by the hour, as does mine. Ginny, Dylan, Hannah, and I went maybe a little too hard at Four Square, but it was actually fun. It reminded me of the good old days of playing Four Square in elementary school.

I had forgotten the rules of Four Square, though. It had been since elementary school since I last played. I remembered how there was a King or Queen as the 'winning square' but couldn't remember the rest of the names for the three other squares. Ginny was there to set us all straight. We ended up using in order from best to worst square, King, Queen, Princess, or Squire (I can't remember) and the famous Poop Deck. The internet says it's supposed to be King, Queen, Joker, and Beggar. That arrangement makes a little more sense when you think of royalty. Although, the poop deck was way more fun to yell at each other whenever one of us landed there. I liked our arrangement better.

While we were getting ready to play, I got a flashback of myself, my best friend, my crush, and another classmate playing back in the day. We got so wound up over Four Square and tetherball. Tetherball was my favorite. I remember us screaming, "Cherry Bomb!" as we'd smack the bouncy ball as hard as we could, hoping we'd get an opponent out.

Bittersweet once more, but Dylan leaves tomorrow, and Ginny does too. Ginny is the one who first made me feel comfortable and inviting, followed by Sam, Dylan, Shayla, and now Hannah. After the George situation, I finally voiced again that I would appreciate a single room. Not just because of Sandy snoring and sleeping all day, but because in situations like that, I need to be alone and not hear shit like that. Somehow, it worked!

I'm in my single room now. I just got out of the shower and am now journaling on this joke of a resting place before bed. They seriously need to look into fluffier cushions and thicker walls…Even in my single room, I can still hear my neighbors snoring their dreams away. I still feel so much more comfortable being alone, though, so I'm not going to complain. My sound machine and ear plugs should block out the wall, right? It didn't, but I still slept much better.

It's five minutes to midnight, and the Benadryl that they gave me hasn't kicked in to help me sleep. I think tonight I'll sleep a million times better than last night. It's hard falling asleep in this place. Waking up feels similar. Your last or first thought is usually something like, "Oh, good morning again, mental hospital," or "Okay, let's try and get some sleep in this place and hope we don't hear any snores or screams." I know I'm where I need to be, though.

I've already learned so much and have so much to take home with me. I got calls from six people today. Mom, Dad, my two sisters, my best friend and my boss. Again, I can't believe the support I've been blessed with. I almost and did feel guilty for the amount of calls I received when some people here got none. Is there a class here to help me not feel so guilty all the time?

It doesn't seem fair. For someone to have such a demonized disease without any support. Those people are the strong ones. Anyone with any type of mental illness is a badass warrior. Let me add I just think it's incredible how some manage to stay afloat without any support at all. I completed a full day, did as much as I could, and took so much from the day. We can only go up.

There were things I learned today, however. The Snowball Effect of Thoughts, Feelings, Behaviors, Habits, equal you was super informative. Sometimes, in certain situations, some triggers make you think, feel, or do something in a certain way. For example, if I were thinking, "I am always depressed; there is no hope for me," I would soon after not feel good and be more depressed, etc.

Now, because I am feeling this way, I will probably lay in bed and do nothing as my action. What will my next thought be?

Probably something like, "I'm such a piece of shit. All I do is lay around in bed." Now, how do you think you'll feel? The circle keeps going until *you* tell yourself to *stop* it and/or find the trigger that caused it.

Sometimes, it's difficult because depression can just start as a feeling. There was nothing that per se happened. In this case, your next step, your behavior or action, must be positive. This is the hardest step, getting out of that feeling.

Getting out of bed, going outside for that walk, going into the kitchen instead of being holed up in your room. Even taking that walk to the bathroom can be a win some days. Simply start slow, sit up, relax a bit, and after this, try and get a list of things to do. (Look at pages 131-135 for a list of positive coping skills when not knowing what to do with yourself.)

We also discussed two more common thinking distortions. The first one we discussed was overgeneralization. Overgeneralization is when the distortion differs due to a tendency to perceive a global pattern of negatives on the basis of a single incident. It draws a conclusion about an entire group, topic, or place-based upon insufficient evidence. A great example of this would be, "I had a negative experience in one relationship; I am not good in any relationship."

The second common thinking distortion we discussed was Blaming. Blaming occurs when you focus on the other person as the *source* of your negative feelings and you refuse to take responsibility for changing yourself. An example could be, "I was driving ten miles over the speed limit when I was pulled over by a police officer who parked in a non-visible area on the road. I blamed the officer for setting a trap," or "He makes me feel bad about myself."

On the goal sheet, I worked on my second subject of concern… effective coping. I was given more examples of positive coping skills and positive ways of thinking when faced with a situation. Understanding the common thinking distortions has genuinely made a difference in how I think. It's stupidly interesting why we do the things we do.

xoxo- from KayJo in psych unit B

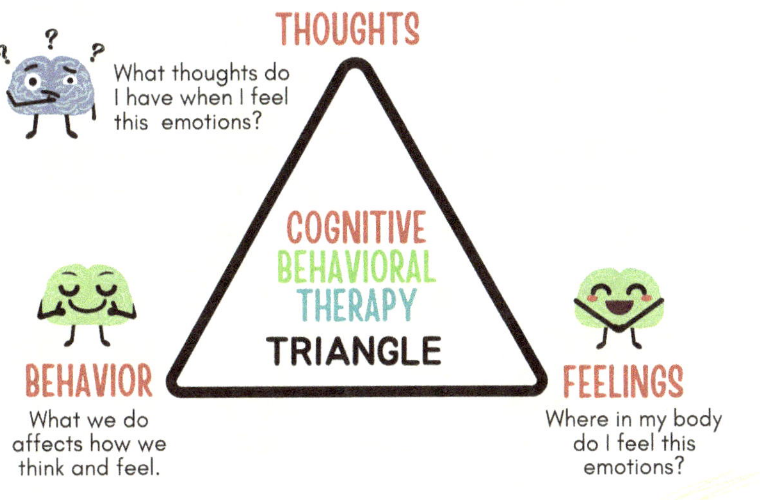

Second Full Day

I t's almost 4:00 p.m.… I've been bad about writing today. I'm not sure why, but I feel guilty about that. I feel guilty for a lot of things, if I'm being honest. I've had lots of individual meetings with doctors and psychiatrists. I went to the fitness group, biked four miles, did some yoga, and stretched. After the fitness group, I've been chatting at a table where Hannah and the new girl, Ava, were.

Ava is super sweet. She is twenty-seven and has short brown hair with hazel eyes. I can't help but remember thinking how beautiful her lips were. I mean, we're in a hospital… no one has makeup here, and it looked like she had plumping lipstick on. I remember thinking of how beautiful she is. Her slight build and at around 5'4 in height carried her timid self over to our table and asked to join us. I said of course. She had a cozy turtleneck and leggings on. She has insomnia and anxiety. She sleeps around two hours a night and makes me feel normal about my insomnia. She also has been told she's Bipolar in the past, but the doctors here disagree.

Last night, I actually slept like a boulder, not a rock. I slept in 'til damn near ten a.m. It felt amazing to catch up on sleep. Maybe that Benadryl did something after all. Again, I feel a bit bittersweet about Dylan and Ginny getting discharged. It's weird how time feels here. It is so precise and on the dot while also so slow and dragging on like there is never an end to it. I've only known them both a little over a day, yet I feel so connected and torn they have to go.

Obviously, I'm so proud of them and wish them the best. It's undoubtedly different leaving this place. Who knows if you'll ever see these people again? Most likely not.

As for Dylan, I was able to stop and give him a hug, tell him he felt like my father figure in here, and wish him well. I told him to take it day by day and that he's got this. He's going down to part-time, which I think will be good for him and his health.

Sadly, when I was in my meeting, Ginny got discharged, so I never got a chance to say goodbye. I did get her number, fortunately. I'm going to miss her energy and charisma, with fun facts flowing out of her constantly.

I told myself I was going to try to be that light for the newbies and others here. I'll never forget that bright, petite redhead with the brightest blue eyes and freckles filling her porcelain skin. We had so many amazing talks and fun in such a short time.

The meeting with the old psychiatrist is going exceptionally well. I tell him my whole life story.

Including all my past traumas, all of my past boyfriends, and "situationships" with any boy. I share about the rape and what changed me forever.

Explaining your whole life to someone is exhausting yet invigorating. We do many 'tests' as he asks me questions. He's continuously rating or writing something down about what I had just answered or said. I wish I could see his paper. We talk about everything. Childhood to now, with everything in between.

We discuss my PTSD and past trauma with rape.

Clearly, this conversation is not an easy one to have.

For a moment, it felt like I was sitting back in my parents' room, telling them for the first time. I hadn't really brought up any of those memories since. I wanted them to stay stored away, hidden.

I honestly didn't realize I was a rape victim until being told I was. I knew some situations were forced, uncomfortable, and nothing that resembled love. Still, I just thought lots of types of relationships go through this. I was so young and naive.

I explained a situation that had just happened that had made me uncomfortable, and my mom just stared at me plainly and asked, "Does this happen often?" I answered, "Yes and no, it depends if we've been drinking, but it's happened sober too, I guess…but I allowed for it to happen, Mom."

She stared at me blankly with glazed-over eyes and took a while to find her words. This is when I got the inkling something wasn't right. She finally choked out, "Honey, that's rape. If you say no and they proceed, that's rape. No matter who it is. You're getting raped." Then, my dad was brought into the room.

I'll never forget the look on either of my parents' faces, but my dad's still haunts me. He was redder than I'd ever seen him with glassy eyes, just listening. I still can't believe his self-control in that whole situation. I didn't come to understand how terribly this boy had treated me until I was told by another. It took me a long time to come to terms with what happened, but finally, it all hit me. I accepted it. Then, I could work on healing from it.

It's hard enough to go in the back of my head, in my special locked box where I've been keeping these memories, even for a second. But to open this locked box and let all the memories come alive again? To speak about what happened to me in detail…No, thank you.

To protect me, some of the memories and occasions are so blacked out and hidden. I had to keep apologizing to the doctor as I'd just bawl when a memory would wiggle its way out into the air. I'd sit back in awe at what I was able to store away.

I keep going back to one memory I can't ever forget. That first time. This memory plays over and over on repeat, as loud as it can in my head. Especially once you start talking about it and bringing the story back to life. Sometimes, randomly, this memory will haunt me. Mostly, it's anytime someone brings up the word 'rape' or 'sexual harassment.' For some reason, my brain can't fizzle this memory away. I can't tuck this one back into that special box. This memory is underlined, bolded, and italicized.

My brain keeps trying to make me slip away into a world of numbness and disassociation. Thank God, the doctor kept me straight as he knew this is what happens to victims of rape when talking about their traumatic memories. He made the whole experience doable, as comfortable as a conversation of trauma can be. I wouldn't have been as open if I were with someone with whom I wasn't comfortable enough to open up to. I'm glad I got the doctor I did. This all needed to come to the surface, as hard as the conversation was.

I remember everything from that night. I still smell his cologne. I remember exactly where we were. What comforter laid on us. What I was wearing. It's all thrown away now. I remember saying, "No, not tonight," and then proceeding to get probed anyway. I remember fighting back someone <u>who I thought might</u> <u>love me</u>, trying to get him to stop. Only to have my head smashed into the pillow to shut me up while he proceeded. I wonder if I'll ever be able to truly forget the details and overall experiences I endured with this person. Probably not, but it's something that has made me into the strong woman I am today. Something I can say I am a survivor of.

We also discussed my head trauma at the age of sixteen in a solo car accident. I was on my way to school, running late. I remember looking at the intersection I speed through daily and then getting distracted by the beautiful sky. All of a sudden, I'm fishtailing. I overcorrect just to overcorrect again. Battling my way across the gravel, I idiotically sped 80-90 miles per hour. God knows how I didn't roll. I then made my way into the ditch. There was an approach only a few feet ahead of me. With no time to think, I held on for dear life as I smacked that approach. I went airborne about 100 feet only to knock myself out and break my windshield with my head.

You know, in the movies, when everything goes slow motion, when there's a dramatic fall or crash?

Yeah, that happened. My life flashed before my eyes, and my last thought before smacking my head was, "Wow, this is it." I woke up in the passenger seat completely unscathed, besides my severe head trauma. That's the other wild thing, without my seatbelt on, how didn't I eject from the vehicle? Just another one of God's mysteries that I'm grateful to look back on and say I made it through that, too.

He told me that some of my issues may get worse over the years as I've had severe head trauma. This isn't the first time I've heard this, but it's always so encouraging to get reminded. (Obviously, sarcasm.) Although he says it's only a possibility and something we'll only know until we know. He gives me great advice and peace of mind about the future. I just need to remember that this is my life. This is my path. All the little details will fall into place.

We could have talked for hours. He felt like a version of my grandpa, 'Papa,' who had passed away during my sophomore year of High School back in 2015.

Every time he giggled, I think I glowed a little, imagining my Papa sitting across from me. Telling him my whole life story and experiences while he tries to decipher what's wrong with me. It was funny, too, because he told me I remind him of his granddaughter, whom he doesn't see much of.

It felt surreal. Our talk goes so well that I even have the urge to give him a hug after our conversation, so I do. It feels like I am hugging Papa for a second. Sometimes, I think God does that on purpose. Sends you people who remind you of those you've lost. To make you feel like they're still here. Still around, through other people, things, or places.

Do you ever get that random Deja Vu feeling when you remember something from your childhood or past? It's usually with a loved one who's passed or not in your life anymore. You could simply be at a place where you and this other person once made a memory together. In your mind, it can be merely a little whoosh of a memory.

You either randomly have the thought cross your mind, or you do something that triggers a memory. That right there, I think, is a sign that they are thinking of you. Watching over you. I usually tear up when moments like this happen but smile at the thought of them thinking of me at that exact second. Believe what you will, but I think those moments are more than they appear to be.

I talked to another psychiatrist today, and he also helped me see the big picture realistically.

We're going to try Zoloft on a low dose while tapering off Pristiq. Pristiq is what I have been taking for my depression over the past six years. I took a low dose this morning and can hardly tell, but I wouldn't be able to tell this soon anyway. Either way, I feel a little brighter and better today. A nurse said from Monday night to Wednesday, I am shining already.

It's crazy what this place is doing. I'm glad I came. I have so many coping skills to add to my toolbox already. I have some decisions ahead that still terrify me, but I think I'll have a clearer mind when I make these decisions.

I genuinely don't feel suicidal today. My intrusive thoughts have been much quieter, with a lot less of them. It's nice. Calming. Damn, and some people are naturally feeling like this? Every day? Huh.

Anyway, I'm not sure if it's being around people who need more help than me, people with no support systems, the staff, classes, or what, but I feel good.

Which is odd to say. I feel hopeful, a strong contrast to the hopelessness I've been feeling for months. I hope it lasts. If it doesn't, I have support, a plan for my meds, and coping skills newly learned. Overall, I have a clearer mind to hopefully pull myself out of my holes more easily.

I'm not going to lie… I'd love a bowl of weed right now, as well as a good old rip of nicotine, but this patch must be doing something because I haven't lost my mind yet. Oh, yeah, update, I am now using a nicotine patch and nicotine gum. Ha. The 'one piece of gum an hour' rule wasn't cutting my addiction. So now, I chew on this burning gum while sporting this sexy patch.

I resent the past version of myself who hit a Juul for the first time. How I wish I never got so addicted. I have such an addictive personality, too, and I knew that. Peer pressure really got to me. My past self would never believe Karlee got addicted to anything. I remember telling myself that I would never let a chemical control me like that. Four years later, here we are. I damned myself at nineteen.

For those who don't know, a Juul is an electronic cigarette that you can put flavored pods into with the pods encasing either 3% or 5% nicotine. They look like a flash drive and are far too accessible to take with you anywhere. The hottest thing on the market when I was nineteen was Juul. Mango and Mint pods were everywhere. Now, ever since the FDA took away the good flavors, Vapes are back.

It was strange being in college without some sort of nicotine device. Not to be that person, but everyone had one and was doing it. Seriously. It was brand new in the world, so everyone was *at least* trying it out. It was like you were the loser who didn't vape or 'The

God' who didn't. It just really depended on who you surrounded yourself with.

My group never peer-pressured me. We, unfortunately, all already had the same addiction when we moved into our house together. This obviously wasn't helpful for any of us. When one of us would hit our Juul, the rest of us would want to hit our own. The cycle continued.

Multiple times, we'd make pacts about quitting as a house. Sign fake contracts that said we'd get bitch slapped if we were the first to cave, got tackled when we tried leaving to get more pods for our Juuls, guilted each other, gave each other shit for finishing off another pod, etc.

We truly did try for some time. Suddenly, it's like we all mutually gave up and gave in to our addictions. Got tired of slapping each other and lowkey making each other feel guilty when we had the urge to hit our own nicotine, too. It made us all feel like hypocrites in a way. We wanted to remain friends and not let our addiction and urge to quit be what breaks us.

That's one thing. The other was that we were in college. College pertains to a few things: studying, socializing, changing, and partying. When did we hit our Juuls the most? When we were nervous and anxious studying or out drinking and partying. It was a vicious cycle. You'd try quitting and you'd go to socialize and see it everywhere. Even blown in your face because it was that normalized and common. In addition, you'd go through another change in life and have the angst to grab that Juul for a calming rip. It felt impossible to quit. I'm jealous yet so proud of those who have the willpower to quit cold turkey.

I now understand the commercials about how hard it is to quit. Good on you if you have quit or are working on quitting vapes or any type of nicotine. I'm truly proud of you. I genuinely wish I never hit that Juul for the first time in the hallway of that house party.

We rarely smoke cigarettes. We let our guy friends handle that. More times than we'd like to admit, our dumbasses let them smoke cigarettes in our house. Lordy, we couldn't get the smell out of there fast enough. We'd be hypocrites if we said we didn't hit a cig with them a time or two. We rarely could ever finish a whole one ourselves. Moreover, we didn't want to finish one, or should I say we couldn't. We'd usually share one cig amongst the four or five of us girls.

This may be weird to say, but it was kind of wholesome, letting the boys smoke inside. They were so happy and content. Especially in the wintertime, they were extra grateful. Whenever we'd let our guy friends do this, we'd usually spark a conversation about how this was, how it was back then. Smoking all the time.

Smoking everywhere and anywhere. Both genders. How times have changed with research.

Sometimes, when we were drunk, we'd pretend we were rich golden girls from the olden days who smoked. We'd go and bum a cig off a guy strictly for one or two hits, then we'd later stomp on it like we had 100 waiting for us in our purses. The looks on the guys' faces were always priceless. We'd usually run away giggling to get pizza or get in our Lyft home.

Ugh, how I miss college. I miss my girls and guys and our cute little house. The guys didn't live with us, but it felt like it. Vice versa with their house once they got one the following year. Then, our hangouts weren't always at our house but mixed with the boys'. We always loved coming together for meals. There was always a head chef on the girls' and guys' side. It wasn't me. The guys also got really hyped up when they got to cook, so it was fun watching how they'd prepare a meal, too. It was super fun when they let the gals join in on cooking, but we usually enjoyed the break.

I miss having my best friends only steps away.

Always having a carpool buddy to run the smallest errand. The nature trail walks with the dogs. I look back and think, did I live that chapter to its fullest? My answer is always, "No, but you tried." I kept my motherly nature throughout college as my hangovers got worse year after year. I now know that that was due to my stomach issues, which are now solved. Thank you, Dr. Helder.

I took advantage of my time at college. I took advantage of having so many spikes of dopamine surrounding me. It felt like there was always something within arm's reach that would help spike our dopamine levels. My friends, parties, social events, school events, and, of course, our random spontaneous nights no one could have planned. We had a hit of dopamine nearly daily. Of course, we had our depressive episodes, seasons, and situations. We had each other to help us get ourselves out of each other's depressive holes easier. I'm very grateful for the people I got to live with and the people I met throughout my college years.

Whenever I'm in a depressive state, I almost always end up at the bottom of some dark hole with light above me, too far to reach. At least, it seems impossible to achieve. More times than not, it feels like you're in a hole with water slowly filling it up as you try to stay afloat and alive. It's as if you're sitting below the world, watching it continue on without you as you bask in darkness or simply try to stay afloat and alive. Sometimes, the most important and vital people are not just those who helped you get out of that hole but those who actually take a dive down into your hole with you. Sometimes, you just need someone to sit with you and let you know everything is going to be okay. Simply another person to really listen. Not to discredit those who stand above your hole encouraging you to climb on up, but sometimes we need someone to take that scary dive with you and help you climb your way out willingly.

I had these people in college. I still have a few to this day, thank God. But this is no easy task to do. If any loved one, partner, best friend, family member, or simply acquaintance takes part in this, it'll affect them too in some way or another. It's THOSE people who you need to remember who was really there for you during your times of drowning in your hole.

Anyway, overall, college was great. Eye-opening in the most beautiful and disastrous ways. College went by too fast. It felt like in a flash of a single year, three and a half years got squished together. All the friendships, all the lessons, all the new first times, all the crazy nights, all the adulting things—all the memories are cherished in my mind.

I have to rest before cognitive behavioral thinking and goals group. My homework is all done, though! I lay my head down on a pillow that feels like it's stuffed with newspaper and pull the lightest sheet over my body. I had to ask them for a blanket because, well, come on. I'm consistently an ice box, and that sheet? I'm not sure what that was, but it should not qualify as a linen of any sort.

It feels like I'm in self-love and self-care school. I wish I could come more often to continue to grow and learn more. Maybe someday I will be back, and that is okay. I'm immensely glad I got started on my journey now. This isn't an overnight thing. It takes practice to train your demonized brain, but it is possible. It's an ongoing process. I'm glad I got started on my journey now rather than pushing it off for more years.

Personally, I think your mental health is the most important thing. It's something I try to train daily. But how can we expect ourselves to physically do what our mindset wants without the energy or desire to do anything at all? We need to have our mindset and mental health straight before we try to attempt nearly anything.

This is the most essential aspect of yourself you need to come to terms with. Whether that's putting your pride to the side, accepting you have an issue, and trying to work on it. If you're aware you may have a mental illness, for your well-being, it's time you start the journey of figuring out yourself and your self-love. *You can do it.*

I'd love to thoroughly wash my face and hair, by the way. This 'two in one' baby shampoo and conditioner, along with no face wash, has been a struggle. Not to mention this three-inch toothbrush they gave us…*What is this?* I understand the 'normal' toothbrushes could be used as a blunt force object and an electric toothbrush…well, the batteries…however, this has to be a joke. I use my index finger and thumb to hold onto the tiny brush and about fist myself every morning and night. But hey, at least they gave us something to brush our teeth with, right? It's all temporary, though. I should probably mention that the mirror is also painted…obviously…? The toilet also doesn't actually have a seat, so we can't use it to hurt ourselves or others. I tried hanging my towels last night after my freezing shower, but the racks all have shelves *in* them. Again, so we can't hang ourselves. Everything in the room, everything we were given, was baby-proofed. Suicide proofed.

I had a scary, hanging dream last night but cannot remember it too well. All I know is I was almost hung. Huh. Probably from thinking about the shelves or something. So, that's weird, but again, I feel better and more hopeful. Until tonight…

xoxo- KayJo from psych unit B

NIGHTLY THOUGHTS

NOVEMBER 30, 2022

It's 10:25 p.m., and I am not doing well. I'm not sure what happened. I had a great day. I've had great talks with doctors and psychiatrists, and plans have been set. All of a sudden, around 6:00-7:00 p.m.. I've been going downhill. I talked to my big sister before the eight o'clock goals group, then my little sister at 9:00 and 9:45 p.m.

I'm not sure if I'm homesick or what. I just bawled on the phone with my little sister, worrying about the big steps I need to take when getting out of here. I'm worried about work, when to return, and whether that time will be fair and appropriate. I feel selfish in so many ways.

I feel guilty for my boyfriend and putting him on hold for damn near four months. This doesn't feel fair to him at all. I told him not to wait, but what if I regret that later? What if he is my guy, and I'm ruining any future we could have? It's all so hard. I don't want to hurt anyone, let alone someone who's loved me the best thus far.

Soon after, my mind trails to the issues. What if there's someone who could handle and love me better? That seems impossible. Like I said, he's loved me the hardest, the fullest, the best love I've experienced.

Maybe the best love I'll ever experience. Perhaps it'll be the love I constantly look back on and regret when I chose my self-love over our relationship. Who knows.

He's over there thinking I'm going to come out fixed and run back home. I know I shouldn't do that. I'm not ready to immerse myself back into my old life when there are so many uncertainties with myself, yet.

I know I'd get pulled for a one-on-one after bawling in front of the whole staff. Dr. Jean Claude came to check on me and reminded me that I'm in the right place, and that my support system is off the charts, as many have no one.

I know I'm fortunate. I know I'm blessed. I know I'm loved. Why do these demons defeat me so brutally at night and at the most random times? I cannot grasp my head around how someone so fortunate can feel so defeated, hopeless, and alone. When I'm not alone. Others here have it so much worse. While others, I tend to 'beat' with my issues.

I've ruined any future I could've had with my boyfriend with what I'm putting him through. I feel like I've gone back ten steps without any warning or any reason. What happened from my optimistic day and feeling of maybe getting discharged tomorrow? The whole staff watched me fall apart. There's no way I'll get out tomorrow now. I guess I'm not as ready as I thought, and that hurts. It disappoints me.

I know I'm in the right place, but I thoroughly want to go home. At the same time, I almost don't because of the decisions and plans that need to be sorted. It took me seven months of rape and all forms of abuse to finally end another, older relationship because I didn't want to hurt him.

How do I break up with someone who truly loves me? The good, the bad, the terrifying. How is he still here now? Like he said, "I won't wait years." What if me, myself, and I need a year? Life is so short, and you can never get back time.

All the doctors, family, and friends say it takes time, but I feel like I'm wasting it away. As I waste time, I feel as if I'm also taking everyone's time and love for me with them. How can everyone stay so patient and kind with me? They have to be thinking, "Okay, enough is enough. Let's go!" And I agree.

Maybe talking about my past, past traumas, and overall, what I'm going through with the doctors, nurses, and staff triggered this. Despite that, I felt at peace for a good portion of the day. I got my crisis plan figured out, my medication change is en route, and I learned about new coping skills.

I feel numb and dissociated again. This feeling makes me feel like I'm not real, like I'm not here.

Simply floating in space, stuck on the ground of some structure filled with people. I hate my head. I hate these demons. I'm trying to use what I've gained to help turn off these thoughts, but it's like trying to train a dragon. The classes make it seem so simple. "Just stop the thoughts, tell yourself to stop it and rearrange your brain and thoughts," they say. It feels like I'm learning a new language, for Pete's sake.

I was so optimistic earlier but abruptly crashed down. I keep telling myself that the love and support I have should be enough to rearrange and be okay, but it's not working. I consistently need to keep practicing, but this truly is a craft. A craft I can't seem to understand or stay positive about.

Now, my head is starting to think about others more than myself, which is typical. It's like it's intangible to only think of myself and what I need. All I do is immerse myself in those I love and their problems. Their feelings over mine. Maybe I've developed this into a coping skill. I've been doing that for twenty-three years, and I'm expected to rearrange that mechanism in under a year? How?

I'm depressed. I'm anxious. I'm worried. I'm scared. I'm a fake. I'm a fraud. I'm a terrible human. I'm all over the place. I feel like my life is a hoarder's house that can't be cleaned.

I hope tomorrow is an entire good day. Still, half a good day is something I'll repeatedly take over a whole bad day. My eyes and head hurt. Let's hope I get some sleep tonight. FUCK.

Here are the <u>things I did learn today, though...</u> The two common thinking distortions I learned about today were *Magnification and Discounting the Positives. Magnification* is when people blow a situation out of proportion to reality. Making a mountain out of a molehill. An example of this can be, "A car pulled out in front of me on the way to work. He was trying to make me late for work and ruin my whole day!"

Discounting The Positives is when you're looking at our past positive accomplishments or qualities and finding reasons why they are false. An example could be your friend telling you she loves you and you are beautiful, but your thought is, 'She is just saying that because she is my friend.' One final example of Discounting The

Positives could be you spill a glass of milk. Instead of it being a minor annoyance, it becomes a major upset that ruins your day.

On our goal sheets, I worked on my final subject, recognizing choices and alternatives. This is when I was given homework of choices in certain situations to pick from. This was also when they made me work on affirmations about myself. I suck at self-affirmations. I couldn't even finish a list of twenty things I like about myself or am good at. This was a good exercise to work on, for sure. (See pages 136-141 for a list of positive affirmations I was given at the hospital for anyone who needs a little pick me up when they're down.)

-NO xoxo from KayJo in psych unit B

At the end of this chapter, I refer to myself very negatively. These were raw, genuine emotions I was feeling and believing at the time. I am aware these are not positive ways to speak of myself. I do not encourage this way of speaking of oneself. Whenever I think like this now, I dig out the positive affirmation sheet I was given at the hospital. (See pages 136-141 for a list of positive affirmations.)

Third Full Day

December 1, 2022

It's 7:20 pm, and I am writing this with a green pen. My girl Hannah stole it from the Art Therapy group for me, which makes me smile. She calls me her Güera (white girl), and I love it. She hates white girls because her boyfriend cheated on her with a "white tweaker." She assured me I'm the *only* white girl she likes. She said she considers me a friend now, and I am with her. I love her and her energy. She often makes me forget where I currently reside.

We've been keeping each other sane, making jokes, and keeping everything as light as we can. We use a ton of dark humor. Maybe a little too much, but hey, I have to cope somehow. Some of the other patients don't get it or get us. I'm not sure how I'd be without her.

We've been pushing each other to go to this and that when one of us doesn't feel like going.

Today's been a good day. I hope the night continues that way. Lil Nug came and surprised me with a visit. It was so good seeing and holding her. She stayed for an hour but had to leave at 7:20 p.m. We got an extra 20 minutes because of a lovely nurse. I cannot believe she drove an hour and a half to come see me for one hour. I'm blessed with the best.

I continue to feel guilty about getting more calls, and now a visitor when some people here don't get either. But me, being my empathetic self, I can't help feeling that way. I'm immensely grateful for the cards I've been given. It's hard to imagine who or where I'd be without that.

Wow, writing is so much easier and more fun with a pen! Damn. A dude recently did a room check and didn't even notice I have a pen, which makes me laugh out loud. No worries, journal, not going to kill myself with it. I love it too much. Oh, yeah, and myself too.

I had multiple talks with techs, staff, and three new doctors today. Dr. Hanigan asked me about how I was doing. I was honest about last night and how I've been feeling. I assured her that I had my crisis plan figured out and had so many skills to take with me in my toolbox. She asked if she thought I'd be ready and okay to get discharged tomorrow, and I said, "I think so?"

Having my medications on a new track gives me hope. I told her that as well. Still, I won't know for at least a couple weeks if they're the right fit anyway.

Even if I had been here the entire ten days, I still wouldn't know. I'm eager to see if these meds will help me this time.

I've been to all the cognitive behavioral therapy (CBT) sessions, as well as both fitness and music/art therapy classes today. They went well. In CBT, we did *"magnification"* as one of the common thinking distortions we use. I wrote about the situation of a good friend blocking me.

I didn't share aloud but asked the instructors to stay back and talk to me about it, and they certainly helped. They think I may be magnifying and blaming, but more blaming a certain someone for how they are making me feel. The nurse even said that this distance could be good for both of us. When and if the time comes where I see them in person, that would be the time to say, "Hey, that really hurt and confused me, but I'm glad to know you're okay."

I wish I didn't love as hard as I do. I have loved people for years and years without them knowing. All I want is for those in my life to be happy, content, and okay. I simply want to be able to be back in some people's lives that I've lost along my journey. I miss so many people.

In music therapy, I requested *The Night by Morgan Wade*. I was so happy to hear it. As you know, I can't have my phone, the radio, or anything, so hearing my favorite song was way too much dopamine for me. The instructor even thanked me because the song was powerful.

We drew a mountain with our successes and a valley with our lows, and it was *not* easy. The music did help a lot. Afterward, in art therapy, we were given a silhouette of a person and told to create something out of it.

The one I chose looked like someone thinking hard. I put them on a cliff with fire and a black hole below them. Next, I drew a golden ladder going up to the sky, with him in the gray area. His body stayed white to show feeling empty and numb, with his head blue to signify his blue, sad state.

I saw it as me or anyone who has depression, Bipolar Disorder, or whatever it may be, and how you can choose to take a dive in your hole, stay numb in the gray area, or try to climb up to the heavens and the good. I got a lot of compliments on it.

Jared is new but has been here before. He voluntarily checked himself in for reasons I'm still unsure of. Sounds like he was running away and decided not to and came here instead. He's shorter, yet still taller than me by a hair with a medium build and arms that could knock you out in a swing. He looked powerful. His smile was very affectionate and made others smile whenever he flashed his pearly whites.

His dark hair matched his eyes, but there was the oddest thing about his eyes. I think it was how his dark eyebrows sat, but he always looked like he was thinking of some devious plan behind this teddy bear persona.

He just had very dark eyes that sucked you in, in a way. Jared has a great sense of humor, including our favorite type, dark. His laugh is affectionate as well as someone always cracks up whenever he does. He's been a great addition to the group.

Melanie came yesterday, and boy, has she been through hell and back! Her arms and neck are covered in slit scars. She looks like she's maybe 80lbs, and her teeth make me think meth may have been a thing for her at one point. That or no dental care ever. She has long dark hair and beautiful hazel eyes with freckles underneath them. She has one of those raspy voices you can't help but love to listen to. Surprisingly, she was twenty-nine, and she had been in and out of hospitals since she was sixteen.

I'm not going to lie. She's surprisingly super outspoken and scares me a little. Let's just say I'm happy she likes me, and I'm on her good side. I love being there for her in any way I can. I love to help anyone in any way that I can.

She had recently lost her baby boy. She delivered, but the poor baby wasn't getting enough blood and oxygen, so he was stillborn.

Shortly after, she drove her car into a hollow brick building and left the scene unscathed. The car and building were destroyed and went up in flames shortly after the ambulance took her tiny body out of the destroyed car. I told her there was a reason for that. Her story isn't done.

She's very much into tarot card readings and did a reading on Hannah and me. They were both scary on point. I met Melanie at dinner last night and got to talk to her and get to know her then. After our conversation, she joined our table a couple hours later. I hope the best for her. She's been great to talk to. I couldn't come up with five more affirmations about myself to the list of twenty for homework, and she spit them out like nothing. It's crazy what others see in me that I can't sometimes.

Since it's the first of the month, there's a rotation in the doctors. This meant all the patients had to retell their stories to the new doctors and psychiatrists on the floor. This was a bit exhausting. Since it's also the first of December, our staff, which we just had for most of our stay, had a Christmas party that night. We all got new nurses, new doctors, and new psychiatrists. This frustrated me a tad as I had finally gotten some of my nurses' and doctors' faces down. It felt like they should be there when I got discharged. But that's just how the rotation goes, and coming in on the twenty-eighth, I was doomed either way with having a switch up.

This really pissed off some other patients. Like the world was melting, pissed off patients. Some of the best entertainment I'd had in a while, honestly.

Watching grown adults throw a fit at other adults just trying to do their job. It was a bit dramatic. Melanie was one of these pissed-off patients. There was a situation where there were at least seven different patients surrounding the enclosed table filled with staff. Some asked where their nurses were, some asked for their usual meds at that time, some crying as their doctor was nowhere to be found, and others yelling at nurses to get them this and that. They'd scream that things were in different cabinets than the ones the new nurses were reaching into.

At one point, I thought a patient was going to leap over the table into where all the staff members were. Thank God no one went that far, but some got close. It was kind of a hot mess. The staff we got gifted were from a different unit, so everything was different for them as well. Everything was in different places. They had to learn about every patient's history and medications. It was a lot to handle if I were to put myself in their shoes. I felt bad for the staff as they scrambled to pick up the pieces that were left for them.

I'm sitting at our table, coloring or doing a word search, then hearing a voice screaming at the staff, "I have literally been here countless times. If you knew the slightest information about Unit B, you'd know my name, know my story, and know where my meds are located!" It was Melanie doing the screaming. She had her toes just across the line, which cut us off from the staff and the living space. She was repeatedly told to back up, relax, and they'll find her meds. In response, she'd yell back, "I am literally not in your space, I am behind the line! I am right behind the line, but I can easily cross it to get to medications if no one can find them," she uncrosses her arms and points towards where they are, persistently tapping her foot in the process, "I can literally see my medications from here!"

Melanie received another warning that tells her to back off once more. She then screams, "This is fucking ridiculous! Give us back the staff we've been working with all week! None of you know what is going on!" She then proceeds to stomp over to our table, like she normally would. I felt uncomfortable as the staff watched where she sat and analyzed the rest of the table. They stare and stare as if they have magical powers and can tell if one of us is going to blow up or cause a similar situation. Melanie shares about what was happening and why it was such a mess, as she's been through this exact rotation of doctors being here on the first of the month a few of the times she's stayed here.

This was a fun little update. I went up to the nurse's station after Melanie had given her piece. I told them I was sorry for all the chaos they'd been handed and apologized for Melanie. They smiled and said something along the lines of, "Yeah, we aren't too thrilled about any of this either, but we're just doing our best." I thanked them for everything, then went back to the table. I'm going to the eight o'clock goals group now and might go try and fuck up some Four Square. Talk to you later…

xoxo- from KayJo in psych unit B (confused & anxious)

New Roommate

DECEMBER 1, 2022

It's 11:00 p.m. I went to the goals group but wasn't feeling the gym tonight, so I didn't end up going. I wanted to shower and do laundry before lights out. God had another plan. I ended up getting to know my new roommate, who got here today instead.

Her name is Jenny, but she goes by Ana. She's in her late thirties, if I had to guess. She has bright blue eyes, a red blushed face, a tiny button nose, and what remains of her hair is bleached. Where her front two teeth should be, she only has her right one. That's it, simply the one front tooth. She told me her family has terrible genetics.

She has nineteen different personalities within herself, and Jenny doesn't come out. First off, she goes, "Hey, just so you know, if I wake up screaming, just ignore me. I get sleep paralysis and will have a panic attack and probably will end up showering throughout the night." I asked her if there was anything I could do, and she said no. I told her I was here if she wanted to talk, and at that instant, her story began.

She wasn't raised the best and was abused, raped, experienced incest—any form of abuse there is, she has sadly known firsthand what it is like. The number of men this woman had been raped by is heartbreaking. Ever since she was four years old, she's developed more and more personalities. I remember a few, but I didn't have my notebook at the time. I wasn't going to be like, "Hold up, can you pour your heart/life out to me *after* I grab my notebook?"

'Ana' is the dominant personality; she is blonde and is sort of 'the mom' of the personalities. 'Tilly' is the mean one who talks in British and takes advantage of Jenny. I was warned that if Jenny started talking in British, I should go and get staff immediately. She told me, "Beware, she wants to set the world on fire." 'Sheila' is a four-year-old who's scared of everything and hides in her room most of the time. 'Quinn' is seventeen and thinks she's going to Brown next year to study mythology. She says Quinn is lots of fun.

'Louis' is bad, makes her an alcoholic drug addict, and has been fighting her for years. Jenny didn't listen to Louis and her demands of stealing drugs and being bad. Louis didn't listen to Jenny when she told her that she was not the parent of her kids and could not treat them that way. After that, Louis disowned Jenny, and she was grateful for that.

'Clyde' protects her when she sleeps "but hasn't been doing his job lately," 'Little Sam' first emerged earlier this week. 'Astrid' is her fun stoner self. 'Vix' is someone we don't want to emerge as well. I cannot remember them all, but I am going to be introduced to and educated about them tomorrow, as the drugs she's been given have knocked her out.

Jenny says she experiences death in all her dreams. She doesn't wake up the second before, like most people, due to her screaming because of sleep paralysis. She used to think she could time travel as she'd come out of a personality and not remember who/where she was or what she did.

Last night, the four-year-old emerged, so she was talking like one to her husband. She was confused and wondering who her three kids were and where she should sleep. Her husband told her she was crazy, so she left and started walking "until her feet bled, she passed out, or died." The cops were called and took her here to Unit C last night, and now she is here in Unit B.

The doctors, her husband, and kids, as well as her friends, all think she's crazy, a pathological liar with an amazing imagination and need for attention. She told me the only one who believes her is her therapist and me. I haven't seen another personality so far, but she told me Mimi is numb and "another name" is nothing, and those two were out today.

I truly believe her. The details, stories, conversations, and arguments in her head of who gets the light. Jenny is usually hidden but feels okay being called that, as that's her real name. Without belief, she gives in and goes with it.

As I continue to write, I'm lowkey waiting for her to scream and have an episode. I'm so glad I sat down and talked with her. She needed to get it out and to someone who believed her and simply listened. We talked for forty-five minutes, and as time went by, it was suddenly time to take our pills. She has been zonked out since.

She says sleep for her is terrifying; it's not relief, relaxation, or good dreams. It's night terrors and sleep paralysis. She warned me she doesn't know who she'll be when she wakes and to be cautious. I'm kind of scared to go to bed. I wonder if it'll happen tonight.

I feel bad. I may be leaving tomorrow just as she has someone she can confide in now. I want to meet these other personalities. I want to make her feel okay and not crazy for having Multiple Personality Disorder, which *is a real thing*. There aren't enough studies and treatment plans for that yet. It's hard to get the proper medication when the doctors think you're lying.

Who knows, maybe she is and has me fooled, but her shaking, trembling, crying, and eye contact of "listen please" makes me feel different. The details she has about every personality are too graphic to make up. She's been silent for years as everyone has told her she's lying and wanting attention. Why would you want that kind of attention, though?

I could tell after our talk that she felt better. I told her that I'd be here to talk and learn more if she's comfortable whenever. Maybe tomorrow. I genuinely hope Tilly or Louis doesn't come out and try to kill me tonight. See what I wrote? I *don't* want to die.

Tonight has been a lot, but so much better than last night. I have big decisions to make when I get discharged, and it still gets me worked up and anxious. I pray and hope my head is clear enough to do those things strongly and be somehow okay afterward.

I simply don't want to hurt my boyfriend. I don't know if I can. He even said he wouldn't know what he'd do if that happened, and that terrifies me. I think "not now" is still my choice. I feel like if I break up with him, I'll be losing my greatest love, my best friend, and any chance of a future with him when the best version of Karlee is here.

I'm still trying to put myself first, but it's so hard when I think about the pain I'll cause to so many people. I'm going to shatter his light. The best part about him; what drew me to him. I don't want to lose him. I can't imagine my life without him, but I cannot settle for this version of myself.

He deserves the best, the absolute best love. I can't portray that right now, and I don't know when I can. I hate not knowing. I hate feeling like everyone's going to expect me to come out of here "fixed" and "happy." I'm working on it, and this place has helped me so much with coping and understanding myself and my thoughts.

However, depression never leaves. It's like a second personality of mine, and I don't know when she'll emerge. I'm not sure if going home is the best thing thus far, but my goal sheet and coping skills are complete and fixated.

I hope everyone will understand and not resent me for how long I've been taking and how long I still might have. I hate not knowing, but that's the beautiful mystery in life, I guess. I'm going to try to get some sleep now, and I wish myself luck. Everything happens for a reason.

What I learned today in CBT was about Mind Reading and Emotional Reasoning. Mind Reading is when you use your perception of body language or past experiences to believe you know what someone is thinking. An example: A friend of mine passes me on the street and does not say hello. I begin to think, "He is just ignoring me. He does not like me anymore." Emotional Reasoning is when you assume that because we feel a certain way that it must be true. This could look like, "I feel overwhelmed and hopeless. It means that my problems are so big that they are impossible to solve. There is no hope for me."

-xoxo from KayJo in psych unit B

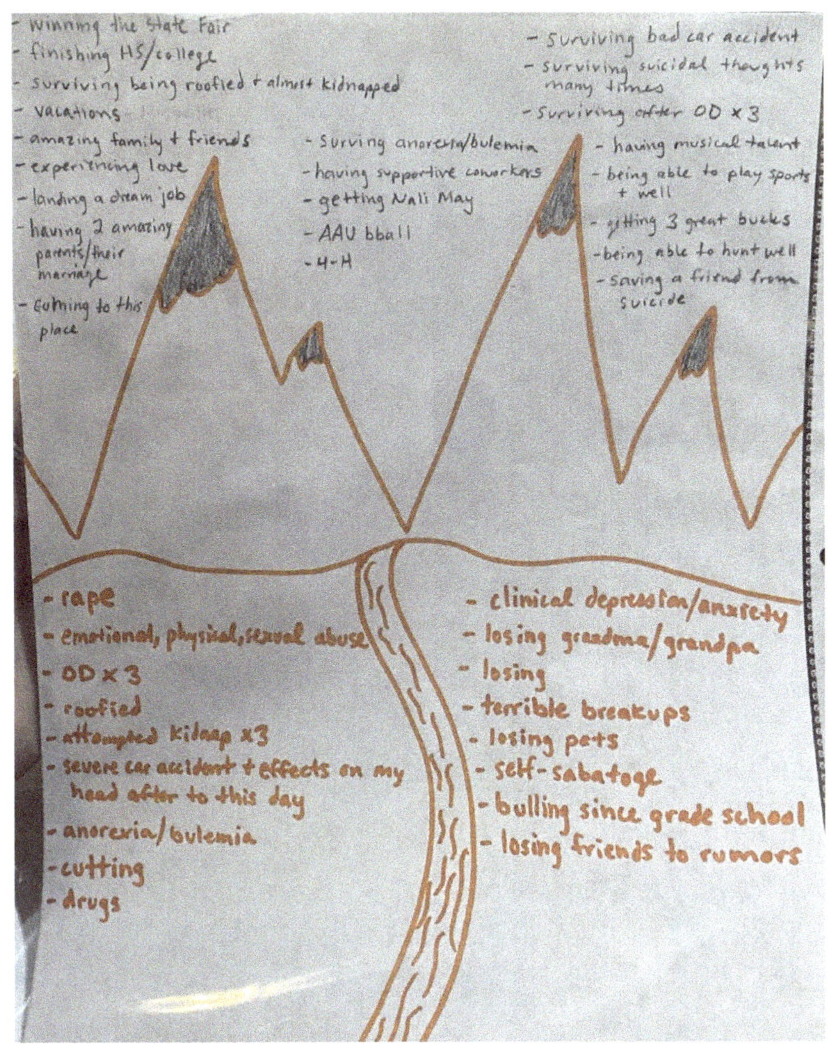
- winning the State Fair
- finishing HS/college
- surviving being roofied + almost kidnapped
- vacations
- amazing family + friends
- experiencing love
- landing a dream job
- having 2 amazing parents/their marriage
- coming to this place
- Surving anorexia/bulemia
- having supportive coworkers
- getting Nali May
- AAU bball
- 4-H
- surviving bad car accident
- surviving suicidal thoughts many times
- surviving after OD x 3
- having musical talent
- being able to play sports + well
- getting 3 great bucks
- being able to hunt well
- saving a friend from suicide
- rape
- emotional, physical, sexual abuse
- OD x 3
- roofied
- attempted kidnap x3
- severe car accident + effects on my head after to this day
- anorexia/bulemia
- cutting
- drugs
- clinical depression/anxiety
- losing grandma/grandpa
- losing
- terrible breakups
- losing pets
- self-sabatoge
- bulling since grade school
- losing friends to rumors

Discharge Day

December 2, 2022

Last night went better than I thought. Jenny's horse tranquilizers had her sleeping peacefully with no screaming or sleep paralysis. I'm happy she slept well, as she stressed how much she hates sleeping because it's anything but an escape.

I got talked to right away by a doctor who discussed being discharged today and how I felt about that. In their eyes, I had completed their curriculum. My goal sheet and crisis plan were set. I'd done all the classes and showed growth during my stay, allowing me to be discharged. They told me they'd work on paperwork and such, and I should be good to go by one-ish. I called my parents and told them the news so they could make plans to pick me up.

I spent the morning drawing and hanging out with our little group. Melanie drew me a picture and gave me a tarot card reading that she copied for me to take home. She was super bummed I was leaving but happy for me as well.

This was when I met Kate, a beautiful firecracker who looked like a version of Jenna Ortega to me. She was this tiny little thing, short too. She had long black hair, beautiful porcelain skin, dark eyes, and Jenna Ortega lips, if you will. Not to mention an amazing sense of humor, light and dark.

Kate had gotten extremely messed up last night, with her blood alcohol at 0.28. She crashed her car and didn't realize it until she got admitted (I was told this later). She doesn't remember much, but she knew she made a mistake as she watched her arm bleed. She slit her wrist and arm vertically.

I asked who found her or what made her call 911, and she bluntly said, "You know? I really didn't know what I was doing or why, but then I just drunkenly looked at my six-month-old puppy and thought, I can't leave her... and I really don't want her to eat my corpse."

She was slightly fucked up still, obviously, and told us she didn't remember even getting to the hospital. She arrived when we were all sleeping. I don't know what it was about her, but she passed the vibe check instantly. She was so open and owning of her actions and knew she had messed up. Her dark humor was a great addition to our group.

Hannah and I even joked about asking to stay another night so we could get to know Kate more. I think a part of us wasn't exactly stoked to be returning back to reality and our problems. I thought I'd feel more at peace leaving, but I was anxious, sad, and scared.

I've grown to love the people, the silence, the noise being canceled in my life. It's hard to focus on yourself and reflect on your life, yet this place makes it so easy. I mean, I know that's what this place is for, but it was such a strange feeling not wanting to leave a place I was so scared to enter.

I made copies of some quotes that have helped me and wrote a personalized note to Hannah, Jared, Ava, Melanie, Jenny, and Kate. It meant a lot to them. Jenny came up to me and thanked me. I noticed Jenny conversing with other patients and talking to the doctors even though on day one, she was pissed and said she wasn't participating in anything. So, this was a happy sight to see. I felt bad leaving the day after she opened up to me about her MPD and sleep paralysis. I truly wanted to be there for her and meet and learn about all the different personalities.

It was strange going from craving home, my vices, TV, and my family to not wanting to leave. I spent the morning writing notes for my friends and coloring. After this, I gave the notes to my friends and said most of my goodbyes. The morning went by too fast. All of a sudden, it was time to eat my last meal and go through discharge. This was something I was excited about being a last for me. You know… hospital food.

Before I went to discharge, I was telling my table about how grateful I was to have a little color in my room. They all stopped eating and looked up at me like, "You have color in your room?" I was like, yeah, I have one green wall, and everyone was to their feet like, "Let's go! Prove it!"

I've never seen so many young adults so excited to go look at a green wall. It was a moment I'll never forget. Watching my friends smile at the vibrant wall I was fortunate to have in my room while they lay surrounded by gray. It's literally the little things sometimes.

When I saw my parents, I was dissociated, numb, and sad. I know they didn't expect me to come out skipping and glowing, but I felt bad I couldn't at least fake it. I was happy to see them, but my reality and issues waiting for me made each step closer to the exit that much harder. I dissociated during all of discharge with a knot in my throat, feeling like I could bawl. I felt like I wasn't quite ready to leave. Once we got all my stuff and new medications, we left.

I got my phone back and didn't turn it on. I didn't miss it or want it. The thought of responding to people or talking to people at all is too much. I remember walking outside, taking a deep breath of fresh air I hadn't gotten in five days, and enjoying the sense of freedom. Shortly after, the cars, noises, people, everything put me on edge and cursed me back to reality.

I was overstimulated, and it only got worse when I settled back home. I have to tell my parents to not talk over each other and turn the TV off while we talk or eat because it is killing my head. Everything is killing my head. I was so happy to see my sisters but had to tell one to tone it down more than once. She's a little outspoken and can be a tad bit loud sometimes. Can you guess which sister? I love her dearly, still.

I've been overstimulated before, more than I'd like. I've had culture shock and complete dissociation from everything around me multiple times. However, I'll never forget how hard this overstimulation was.

Those first couple of weeks are blacked out. I don't remember much of it. All I know is it was terrible.

It's like I got depressed leaving and being back. The medication change kicked my ass. I got headaches and nausea like clockwork every day around 4:00 to 5:00 p.m. (I'm still trying to figure that out to this day.) I didn't want to eat anything. I didn't want to do or see anyone. I only replied to Hannah, Kate, my boss, and some family members. I dragged through each day with fog surrounding me.

I didn't even smoke my first night back. I haven't smoked more than two sessions a day since being out. I'm trying to stay as active as I can and don't want to upset my mom or dad.

Some days, I want to smoke away the pain. Go numb. Nicotine is back, but I don't care about it in the grand scheme of things. I'll get to quitting that eventually. Right now, I have other things to worry about.

It's been a long, rough ride, and it's not even close to being finished. Yet, we've made it through a damn lot of bumpy roads. A quarter-life crisis, if you will.

I saw the psychiatrist on the twentieth. Two and a half hours of questions about my life, medical history, past traumas, and all my dark thoughts. She helped me a ton and tweaked a few medications. We also added a muscle relaxer to help my body fully rest. It was a super good and interesting visit. The appointment gave me hope.

She said she'd add in a stimulant a couple weeks later to help me stay awake and alert better throughout the day. That's been something I've been asking for for years, so that made me happy and hopeful. I'll check back in with her on January third (Happy Birthday, Kenz!) and go from there.

I'm now just taking it all day by day and hoping the next day will be better. I'm fighting these demons with all I have. I utterly need to stay strong and hopeful. Most nights, it feels like an army of demons slaying me. One soldier against an army. I hope I get better soon and can get myself on track. *I just want to be happy.*

-no xoxo from KayJo, freshly at home

POST DISCHARGE

It's 10:41 p.m. I'm numb and empty. I keep going in and out of being completely numb and disassociated to feeling everything at once and hysterically bawling. I got discharged from the behavioral unit on the 2nd. It's been a rough transition back to reality and my life.

The medication changes are quite literally kicking my ass. I seem to have energy for a few hours after taking the new medication, but like clockwork, here comes the hurricane. It's been consistent the past three days of hitting a wall of fatigue, nausea, headaches, and overall numbness and depression around 4:00 to 5:00 p.m.

I've been lying down to sleep that away but wake up more numb than before I laid down. I utterly hate and don't understand how they're changing your medications to make you better. Still, it takes weeks for your brain, body—everything—to adjust. It also doesn't make sense how the number one side effect is worse depression and worsened suicidal thoughts on top of fatigue, nausea, headaches, and numbness.

I feel awful for my mom. She's doing everything she can and asking if there's anything she can do to try and help, but I have no answers. I continue to tell her this is how it is and I'm sorry. If I knew something that would flip the switch, I'd have done it years ago. She's so worried. She can't help but ask me if I'm going to do something and cop out. Her reminders to me of the love and support I have are starting to get to me because I am well aware of them.

I hate how much it affects not only me but my mom as well any time I go through a depressive stage, a medication change, or a change in my life. She feels what I feel, sometimes harder. She doesn't have depression or Bipolar Disorder, but when you watch your daughter dive deep into her hole, it's easy for her to get situational depression. *That's a super cool superpower I didn't ask to have. Giving your mom depression when you're already down bad.*

One of my favorite quotes that I think signifies any mother-daughter relationship is this, "Mothers and daughters existing as wretched mirrors of each other: I am all you could have been, and you are all I might be."

The love and support are part of what makes this all so confusing for everyone involved. I feel bad for everyone who cares about me right now, for the worry they feel, and for the feeling of being helpless to help me sometimes. Welcome to my life… feeling helpless and hopeless more than I'd wish on anyone.

I learned so much in the unit and met absolutely amazing people. It's weird to say I kind of miss it. There was silence, no technology, and there was mutual understanding with everyone there, with no explanations or looks of pity and confusion.

I've been extremely overstimulated after leaving the hospital. The decisions and life I escaped for a week are still here. Now, I have to deal with it, cope, and come back to the reality that is my life right now. I miss Brett, my baby girl, my turtles, our home, and our life before. Unfortunately, I'm getting worse before I'll get better.

That's how it goes sometimes.

I'm positively hoping Sertraline is the golden ticket that helps me become more able to deal with issues and everyday things. I'm tired of being shot and sunk into a dark hole where I can hardly see the light. I naively thought as I grew up, this would all get better. I'd be stronger. Boy, was I wrong! Quite the opposite of what's occurring.

I can't stop thinking about the mess I've made of my life. I'm merely a fool. A sick, depressed, confused, anxious fool. Everyone wants to see me since I've been discharged. I appreciate and love that so much. Still, I'm overstimulated and only want to talk to three people and two others I met in the unit.

They've been great to talk to and help me as they felt similar leaving that place. My support system is genuinely patient and understanding. They aren't pushing it by any means, but it still makes me feel like shit not seeing everyone. *Karlee is simply not here.*

I feel like I keep getting worse. They say it'll get worse before it gets better, and I understand that. I can't wait to feel somewhat normal and human again. Counseling should be interesting this week. Maybe she'll send me back. Who knows.

I simply can't fake happiness, interest, or anything right now. Like Morgan Wade says, "Why do the demons in my mind never wanna leave me alone?" Like seriously, *why?* The only thing I've somewhat kept up on since leaving is hygiene, and that's mostly because I love baths.

I'm disorganized, and I have multiple things I need to get done. Even the 'fun' smoking, TV, and piano seem impossible some days.

I played piano today, and it was so good. I need to force myself to play more often. I usually feel better afterward. Piano was my vice before I even knew what a vice was. I'm super grateful I have the musical ability I do and am able to play such an astonishing instrument.

Mom's been decorating for Christmas, and I <u>love</u> that shit, but I feel no interest in helping this time. I want to. I hope I'll find it in myself to do it tomorrow. I wish my mom could relax and sleep. This is taking a toll on her, and it's bad. I feel awful. I want to be her happy China Doll little girl, someone she trusts and doesn't worry about all the time.

I'm trying to plan shit, but when it comes time for the event, I can't do it. Everyone's been so kind and patient with me. I can't wrap my head around it. What did I do to deserve that?

I deeply want to be better. I want to feel interested in my favorite things again. I want the will to live. I want to be happy. I'm going to go and check on Mom and make my way outside for my nightly smoke.

By the way, I have only been doing this once, twice, or not at all since being discharged. It helps me sleep and relax. Sometimes, it brings out emotions I didn't know I had bottled up all day, too. This disappoints Mom, and it hurts me to do that to her, but it's one of the few things that helps me right now.

I hope tomorrow is better. We start the two tablets to equal 100 mg tomorrow for the first time.

Also, we will be on our first day without any tapering off Pristiq, with no Pristiq at all. So, we'll see.

-no xoxo from KayJo at home

NAVIGATING LIFE ONE YEAR LATER

A ton has happened since my last entry. I went to see my psychiatrist on the third. To this day, I still see her monthly. We ended up tweaking my medications around a bit. Nothing too drastic; she simply added in a stimulant. *Finally.* After that, I traveled alone, for the first time, to Hawaii.

I had this trip planned before I entered the hospital as a goal to make it. I met a couple of my friends back in South Dakota who moved there and stayed with them. I chose Hawaii as my first trip traveling alone because I knew anything after that would feel like cake, and they did.

Hawaii was incredibly life-changing. Not to mention breathtaking. The smell there was like something out of an exotic perfume bottle. I kept taking in as many breaths of the air as I could. It was remarkable. I remember grounding myself there and thinking how easy it was to come up with five things you can see, four things you can touch, three things you can hear, two things you can smell, and one thing you can taste. I felt like a version of myself in another life lived in Hawaii. I was so content and at peace there. I went to the ocean and soaked in Vitamin D daily. Not to mention the constant views of God's beauty. It was a little slice of paradise.

What was there to complain about? I also kept excellent company, which kept me optimistic and sky-high. I was having such a fantastic time that I extended my trip. I didn't ever want to come home. Finally, I did. I felt like I was ready to come back to work after my Hawaii trip. I even told my boss I was ready in the Hawaii airport because I felt *that* good about life.

After Hawaii, I had a hard time coming down from my high. Terrible jet lag, depression from leaving paradise, and coming back to reality once again, and then there were my medications. It's as if my body rejected some medications I was on from the hospital after I got back from Hawaii.

It's like the two weeks of adjusting were up, and all of a sudden, now they decided to stop working. I was nauseous, insanely tired, unmotivated, depressed, and had on-and-off manic episodes. I couldn't keep up with myself. After that, I remember disassociating for a couple weeks as I changed medications again. I got sicker than a dog. That's not an exaggeration. I do not remember anything from that time other than my symptoms and sleeping.

Medication changes are now two words that make my skin crawl. They terrify me. There was a point in time during all of these medication changes when I was entirely not myself. I was closet drinking, cutting, and having casual sex purely to feel something. I was risky with my money, interrupting people like I'd explode if I didn't get words out. This was a very new, weird feeling for someone as soft-spoken as I am. I was doing all the wrong coping skills you could think of.

All the self-harm things you can think of, I was doing it.

I was so unwell. Worse than before the hospital at one point. I developed worse insomnia and was having manic episodes daily. Over the past year, I had gradually lost thirty pounds. My driver's license says I'm 5'7 and one-hundred-and-thirty-five pounds. At one point, I was down to the lightest I have ever been, one-hundred-and-five.

I love baths. Baths have continued to be good for my soul. When I was down to one hundred and five pounds, it really hurt trying to bathe myself. My tailbone was so prominent that if I sat wrong in the bath, I'd rear up in pain. I'm positive I cracked it in one of my falls. That's when I had to tell my mom the new issue. She ended up getting me one of those balloon things that babies use to take baths. So, after I got my little cushion, I was good to bathe again. (I can happily say I no longer need to use this.)

I wasn't trying to lose weight. It's like it just all fell off one day. The stress, depression, and anxiety literally ate me from the inside out. It took me months of force-feeding and stretching my stomach to be where I am happily at now, one-hundred-and-twenty pounds. I have found confidence in this new body and have been working on making it strong again.

It was strange developing body dysmorphia, but the opposite of what I had felt my entire life. I was never happy with my weight or body. I was constantly trying to lose weight. On this occasion, when I wasn't trying at all, it all fell off. I was suddenly this tiny, fragile thing, unsure of her own skin again. Insecure being so small. I got so many comments on my body that I developed a borderline eating disorder. The constant weigh-ins to see where I was at isn't good for any human.

I would eat and eat and gain nothing. I remember thinking, "Damn, I totally was one of those people that would scoff when a skinny girl would complain how small she was, and now I am one of those girls people scoff at." It's an exceptionally touchy subject. A hard one to talk about. It's kind of like depression, anxiety, bipolar disorder, or any disorder—you truly can't understand unless you or a close loved one is going through it.

I lost a lot of people in my life during the months of February and March. People who knew what I was going through. People who I never thought would leave are gone. I understand I wasn't myself, but they knew that. That's what really gets me. What hurts the most. People who you think will forever be by your side, like they said, leaving you while you're at your worst. And they know all of this. I had a hard time compartmentalizing this for an excessive amount of time. Sometimes, I still struggle with it.

Nonetheless, I learned that lost friendships and relationships are simply a part of life. People come and go. The ones that matter and understand you will stay. There are so many people in this world we haven't met yet. I also think God takes people out of your life for a reason. Sometimes only for a few seasons, sometimes for good, but it's all for a reason. Unfortunately, I won't know why until I do.

We lost our fifteen-year-old house dog, Buddy, on June 20th. This absolutely set me back. Buddy was there for my first heartbreak, my first nearly everything. I remember thinking the first day we got him how hard it would be to lose him. I remember telling my friends growing up that when Buddy goes, I go. Dramatic, I know. I loved the hell out of that dog. He also filled this void of Nali when I was alone and depressed. He was there for me in my darkest moments. He was there for the biggest battle I'd been through yet while battling his own health.

The house just feels haunted without him now. There's no more clicking of his nails on the hardwood floor, no more having your little shadow following you into every room, no more greetings at the door. Just no more Buddy. I miss that dog so damn much. *I still catch myself getting a jump of excitement when I come home, expecting to see you at the window waiting. Rest in Peace, Bubbas.*

I wasn't Karlee. I'll fully admit that. I look back at my detailed journal entries and gasp at my past self. It's insane what medication can do to you. What depression, anxiety, and bipolar disorder can do to you.

What anything wrong with you can do to you. I was lost in the wind, watching myself destroy my life from above, but I didn't care. I didn't see a future. I saw a day. Every day, I would think of just living for today. Be happy today. In retrospect, you should live like this every day. But not to the extent I did or with the risks I took.

I lived that way for a while. I was kind of on the run without knowing it after losing a couple of genuinely close friends. I wanted to run away from my life, which kept unraveling. I kept thinking that everything happens for a reason; I respectfully just don't know why yet. Yet, to this day, some of those lost friendships are still floating in the air, still waiting for closure.

Closure, which I don't think will come for some of these journeys with people. That's something I struggle with immensely and probably will forever… loss. After losing these people who were so near and dear to my heart and feeling like I had lost myself as well, I resorted to my traveling era.

Traveling became my new coping skill. Until I ran out of money. After Hawaii, I traveled alone to Colorado twice and Miami once. Then, I went to Portland, Oregon, with my sisters for our first sister trip that was planned over a year ago. Most recently, I traveled alone to Florida and was in the Clearwater/Tampa area. Through all of these trips, I gained some sort of knowledge about myself and the world. I came home from each trip with a new perspective on something else. I changed drastically. I started living each day as if it were my last. I didn't care how much money I was spending. I eagerly wanted to be happy, and traveling was fulfilling that.

I missed Brett and Nali along the way, but I couldn't help but feel like the planes and other states were calling my name. I felt adventurous and didn't want to settle back in and act like we were forty years old again. I realized that *now* is the time to travel, see the world, and experience what I wish for. So, I traveled until, like I said, I ran out of money and had to start working again. This was a hard adjustment for me. I still crave traveling. I love it.

Nevertheless, I'll forever be the country girl from a small town in South Dakota. Without a doubt, I'll eventually have that pull to come home. I would like to travel around three to four times a year if my budget allows me to.

In between trips, I would live life as fully as I could in South Dakota. I would attend events I usually wouldn't. I forced myself to socialize. Forgive people I thought I never could. I was somewhat happy.

I was able to visit Brett and Nali while traveling.

I never felt like I truly lost them because, in between trips, I was there. It wasn't until these past six months that I realized how much I took advantage of that. It's something I wouldn't say I regret, but I definitely would have done it differently.

I was able to see friends I usually don't see as I wasn't working and could attend more events. I was social again. My introverted self was blossoming into something new. I wouldn't stretch it to full-on extrovert, but I'd say I made my way up to being half extrovert/half introvert. As the cold settles in, I feel my introverted self emerging. While this other part of me is telling me to get back on that plane and escape this tundra.

I proceeded to think, "When I'm ready, I can go home to Nali and Brett," never thinking he'd back out on his word. Regardless, a lot of time passed. I changed. Brett didn't get to see this new version of me. I was too busy traveling and trying to be happy while also trying to be independent.

He needed to see and hear more from me, and I didn't allow him to. I gave him glimpses, but after losing people that I thought would never go, I was scared he'd leave for good, too. Now, when I'm ready to come home and start over, he isn't. He says now it's his turn to work on himself, and all I can do is respect that.

Many letters were exchanged this past year between us as if one of us was away at war. In a way, both of us were fighting our own wars alone.

It's like the breakup has restarted itself over. We've merely exchanged seats. I don't like this seat nearly as much as the other one, let me tell you. This shit is debilitating. I've grown more respect for Brett as I sit where he sat. I realize how patient, respectful and kind he was to me on my journey. I just want to know what he's doing constantly and be with him already. I'm sure he felt the same at one point, but he gave me my space and respected it as best he could. I'm still working on doing better at this for him.

Brett wants all of my shit out of the house and wants full custody of Nali, as do I. I don't want to move my shit out, but half the house is already done. Now we have Nali to fight over while he has his time to figure himself out. I pray he doesn't take as long as I did.

Mostly, I hope he doesn't forget about me. Move on without me, taking Nali with him.

This is something I've never mentioned, but Nali is a total daddy's girl. When we brought her home at six weeks, I was still working as a veterinary technician while Brett struggled to find work after the pandemic. Due to this, Brett got to train and be with her daily. I knew she'd imprint and attach herself to him, but that's just how the timing worked out for us. I wouldn't have it any other way. Even though it hurts being a second choice. Brett did an amazing job training her into the good girl she is today.

That being said, I've always said I'd never take them away from each other. Their bond is something I crave, yet I glow at it when I witness it. Nonetheless, Nali is a third-generation registered hunting labrador retriever that's full of my family's dogs' genetics. Her grandma just passed away a couple years ago. Her amazingly talented mama Mea still hunts the shit out of any field with Nali's sister, Annie. They're an incredibly fun trio to watch out in the field. They retrieve those pheasants with such ease. *Literally like they're born with it.* With all that mushed together, I have a harder time just letting her go and letting them live happily ever after. I'm her mom, too. I want to watch her grow, too. I want her in my life, too.

I can't wrap my head around not having either of them in my life. It seems so unfair. She is my dog, too. We raised her together.

Who knows how that situation will play out as hunting season approaches. I hope it's civil. I don't want this to be the last memories of Brett and I… fighting over Nali. As of now, we're doing well with co-parenting and keeping things civil. I still hope for a future for our little family of three. I have to let time do its thing. As cliche as it sounds, if it's meant to be, it'll be. I pray and hope it's meant to be.

I am currently single and not looking for anything.

Some people try to date and such, but my heart and headspace are not in the right place for that yet. I'm too busy missing Brett to think about dating another. I'm open to the idea. I'm always open to love. I mean, if I meet someone who smacks me in the face with this love I can't turn down, then that's my story. Yet, I don't foresee that happening.

This isn't a movie. That can't happen to a person twice. Or could it? Brett and I spontaneously met on Spring Break vacation in South Padre Island, Texas, in 2019. We coincidentally only lived forty-five minutes apart and knew of each other slightly. We were both either in relationships or single at the wrong times to ever come together.

We met in a hot tub in South Padre Island. It was actually super romantic for two nineteen-year-olds. Two days later, we told each other we loved each other. I'll never forget how it felt to fall in love on Spring Break. It was this whirlwind of emotions and clicks I had only heard of and seen in the movies. It was like a movie, but it was my life.

We started seeing each other once we got home from vacation and dated for nearly four years. We were so in love. So happy and content. Our happy couple blossomed into a trio with our new addition, Nali May. Nali May is a third-generation hunting labrador retriever and the daughter of my dad's dog, Mama Mea. She has insanely great genetics and has been trained to a T, thanks to Brett. She is one special girl.

She will turn three in February of 2024. Nali May is so loved by both Brett and me, as well as anyone she encounters.

Once we got Nali, we decided to move in together. I was staying at a single apartment twenty minutes away at the time, where they didn't allow pets. Brett was staying with his parents, and we were more than welcome to train and have Nali there. We were and still are so grateful for all the help they've shown with their granddog baby. Brett's parents owned a rental that was empty due to flooding issues the year or so prior. Brett, being the determined, hard worker he is, took it upon himself to completely flip the house so it was livable for us.

After the house was built, like the cute duo we were, he kept working on the structure and construction side of things. At the same time, I decorated the inside to make it homelike. Like the song, *Made A Home by Cody Johnson,* Brett built the house, but I made it a home. We made it a home together. We made so many memories in that little house on the corner. We rarely had our issues, minimal fights here and there. Our system was down pact by the time six months rolled around. He was the cook, the fixer-upper, and I was the cleaner. The overly obsessive cleaner with OCD who *had* to vacuum daily.

We were happily living together with our baby girl, doing the damn thing together called adulthood. Then, this shit called life happened. Some stupid crap went down that diminished the little amount of self-confidence I had. Fights occurred, and I realized I needed to figure out my self-love and care, as well as my overall confidence and self. Next thing you know, the last bit of the fourth year was *this*.

It's hard not to think that my depression and issues ruined this relationship. My depression ruined my happy life. In a way, it one hundred percent did. In another way, it completely rewired and flipped me for the better because of how low I got. During all of this, at one point, Brett said, "I lost my girlfriend to depression," and that absolutely killed me. It's heartbreaking to see how our beautiful run unraveled.

We had our issues, we had our fights, and we had the things we needed to work on. Like any couple does. The reality of it was my depression, self-love, and care are what took so long to figure out. It's hard to forgive myself for the things I've done and the amount of time I've taken. You can never ever get that precious thing back. You can never get back time. Furthermore, it's even harder to shame myself for all the hard work I've put into myself and my love for this life again. It's a confusing, knotted-up mess in my head, I still try to untangle.

I feel numb to the idea of loving someone else. Loving someone else like *that* I should say. I mean, I love so many people. I fall in love so fast, so hard. I love with all I have. Without the one I know I want to be with in the picture, love seems unreal. Intangible. For a while, right after we broke up, I felt like I could love anyone. The next person to step on up, but I stupidly wanted attention and affection. I solely wanted to feel something. I was so lost and confused, but it wasn't until I grew and learned that I came to realize this.

CONTINUING FORWARD

I have been detailing vehicles at my dad's Ford dealership from the summer to the present. All of his detailers ditched on him at the beginning of summer, so it worked out perfectly when I needed to start working again. I enjoy it a lot. I have OCD, so I actually enjoy a dirty vehicle coming in and being able to make it spotless. It's soothing to pop in my Airpods and jam out while cleaning. I intend to work part-time at the vet clinic again soon. I have been waiting to see how this relationship with Brett would play out before committing to this job back in his hometown. That feels a bit invasive.

Update: We had this conversation, and he giggled and said, "Karlee, I would never tell you not to go for something, especially something you are so good at and love so much. I'd be happy for you if you went back to the clinic." …Let me tell y'all I just completed my first half-day back at the clinic. It was absolutely incredible. It felt like I never left. Like I was home again.

I've also been assisting in embryo transplanting with my cousin every other Friday on dairy cows and heifers. My job is to first help load all the artificial insemination guns with the embryos. I then give them their epidural, clean them out for my cousin, and do the paperwork. Cleaning out meaning, gloved up, shoulder deep, cleaning out their shit. This way, it's clean and easier for my cousin to insert the embryos we loaded thirty minutes prior. I absolutely love doing this with my cousin. I learn something new every time we work together. I'm still getting my taste of veterinary medicine, but it's not enough.

I joined an online group called "Irrational Optimists" around the Spring. The CEO and beginner of this group is Jake Youngblood Dobbs. He is an incredible human who simply wants what's best for this crazy world and all the strangers in it. This group represents individuals who strive to better themselves and their lives in the most optimal ways. We focus on five main pillars: health, mindset, routine, relationships, and business. It's a beautiful online community that has become something so dear to me.

After joining this community and family, I realized just how beautiful different minds from different backgrounds, genders, and ethnicities are. Not to mention, I have this new, more beautiful way of viewing vulnerability. The IO community opened my eyes to purely how important it is to connect and learn from people with diverse backgrounds and experiences.

I've even met someone in person from the group that lived in Tampa, FL, during my Miami trip. This group has especially helped me find my purpose. It wasn't until after joining this group that I realized I wanted to share my story and talk more about mental health.

I've now been advocating for mental health this past year. I've finally started speaking up and telling my story. Encouraging others to come forward and tell their stories and talk about these issues that aren't talked about enough.

I made a brand called 'Unwell Warriors' signifying those who have any type of mental illness. Some who are unwell do not see themselves as warriors. However, any person who deals with any type of mental illness is an absolute warrior. That includes partners, family members, friends, and anyone else who is on the sidelines, taking the hits and backlash of you. Those people, too, are warriors. Helping you fight your fight. Overall, I want to be a part of the mental health awareness movement in any way possible. Help stop the stigma around mental health in any way possible. I created a website called www.unwellwarriors.com to expand the brand and get the word out there more about mental health. I dive into merch that, hopefully, people will come to normalize and wear more of. I also do weekly blogs or whenever I feel like it blogs.

I have been sharing some of the things I learned in the hospital, like some of the common thinking distortions we use (see pages 125-128), as well as positive coping skills (see pages 131-135). I've learned things that have helped me, like grounding (page 129), exercising, journaling, writing, traveling, therapy, reading, going for a walk, socializing, coloring, and even praying.

I don't smoke like I used to. I look back at that version of myself and frown. That's what I abused and used to cope with. I'd smoke, nap, eat, repeat. I didn't realize how bad of a stoner I was until I had the tolerance break I did. Being under my parents' roof helped me not jump back into my stoner habits as well. I dabble every once in a while, but it's nowhere near where I was at one point. I'm proud of myself for how far I've come. I have nothing against the plant. I think it's a beautiful mystery God placed on this earth for us to find. I have my medical card and will probably use it again in the future. Yet, for now, I'll settle for spontaneous occasions when I smoke and relax.

Earlier, I talked about how my depression seemed to have been the kicker to my relationship. That's how it feels with every person I've lost. I wanted to talk about how my relationship with my parents has changed. My relationship with my parents has always been a blessing. We've always been close. I wish I could say this past year made us closer, and in a way, it did. However, I couldn't help but feel the tension growing between my parents as I sat in the middle. Living under their roof most of the time, I got a bit coddled. I think they forgot my age and only focused on what was factual about my life this past year.

That's the other thing. They knew everything; they had to. I had to get better somehow, and lying didn't help me. There were many discussions about boundaries, and they almost always ended in someone in tears or furiously stomping away in confusion. That's the biggest thing that's caused the tension, the misunderstanding of it all. I can't imagine having to be my parent. The parent of someone who has so many diagnoses and issues. The parent of the one who tends to get too drunk at social gatherings because she doesn't realize she's coping. "That child" of the family. The silent yet fatally troublesome one. The middle child, if you will.

Throughout all of this, my parents have decided to go to counseling to hopefully better understand my diagnosis, parenting it, and understanding each other better as they navigate it together. I'm happy about this. I'm hopeful they will understand me better. I'm optimistic about them, in general, even considering going to counseling in the first place. A lot of parents wouldn't even send their own children to counseling, let alone going themselves.

I've been through an abundance of experiences this past year. I didn't ever anticipate my healing and self-love to take nearly a year, but it did. Not to mention, self-love can constantly be added to. It's something you can endlessly work on. I sometimes think, "Oh, if I had known he was going to change his mind, would I have gone back and done something different?" Yeah, I would.

I'll never regret being in the hospital, my solo trips, and my growth while being alone. I grew tremendously as a human, daughter, sister, friend, and potential partner someday. I made some mistakes this past year. More mistakes than I ever have in my lifetime combined. As cliche as it sounds, I'm only human. Year twenty-three was my growing year, without a doubt.

I also need to give myself more grace with how badly I react to some medications and how they affect me significantly. I lost a lot of people this past year. I've also learned that with growth comes loneliness.

Sometimes, you need to disappear and go off the face of the earth for your true self to come back and shine.

I disappeared for a while. I did not want to be on this planet anymore, multiple times. Sometimes, those thoughts still come back. Regardless, the cognitive thinking distortions and Cognitive Behavioral Therapy I learned is something I used all year long whenever I had or have suicidal ideation. I use these techniques to this day. The hospital saved me. It's hard to imagine where I'd be or if I'd still be here at all if I didn't go to the hospital.

I kept in contact with a few people from the hospital. I even got to visit and stay with Kate at one point. Hannah and I still need to get together, but with her living in Iowa, it has been difficult to make that happen. Every once in awhile, we'll all check in with one another. Usually, we tell each other how proud we are of one another while giving each other words of encouragement. Those friendships are something I'll cherish for the rest of my life. They are people I'll forever be rooting for from afar. I think and pray for them often. I hope our little group is doing well out there in the real world.

As for how days go for me now, they go exceptionally slowly. It feels like my life is a ball that has suddenly stopped but is trying so hard to keep rolling. I live with my parents, alone at our hunting lodge or with my sister at her house, whichever one I feel like staying at. It's been strange moving out of that house and living on the move. I've tried to adapt as best I can. However, I can't help but feel like my life is such a mess, as my clothes, items, and everything I own are scattered throughout four different places.

I still see my counselor once a week and my psychiatrist monthly. I also have been looking for a more holistic approach to my mental health. I have tried acupuncture multiple times, as well as PEMF therapy (Pulsed-Electromagnetic Field). PEMF is energy that heals. It's energy medicine. But PEMF is also an essential element of health, so it both nourishes and heals, like chicken soup for your biofield or energy body. I've grown, gotten stronger, and learned more in a year than I can even tell you. That's a whole other book. I'm proud to still be here today. To say I made it.

It felt like Karlee had been under a rock for more than half this past year, but she's emerging back. I don't plan on giving up anytime soon, even though some days it feels like the world hates me and I'm sinking further and further into my hole. I know we all can feel that on some days.

However, we have to remember the amazing days filled with sunshine and happiness. Our favorite people, places, and things.

Those are the days we live for. The things we live for. The people we live for.

Don't forget the most important person to live for—you.

I'm proud of you. Keep up the fight. You never know what will happen in the next chapter. We don't know God's plan. We just have to learn to ride the wave he places in front of us. We can't just sit on the shoreline watching those we love splash around and have fun. Eventually, you have to grow some fins and dive in and learn to ride that wave.

Don't you ever forget to enjoy the little things.

They are so precious and priceless. Remember, everything happens for a reason, and you should always, always give yourself some grace during your journey. Wystan Hugh Auden said, "To be free is often to be lonely."

EPILOGUE

NOVEMBER 28, 2023

One year ago on this day, I wasn't back home celebrating my best friend's birthday with her. I was sitting in between my sisters and my parents up front in a car on our way to my stay at the behavioral unit. I always thought that November 28th would be a special day for me because it was my best friend's birthday. Now, this day has received a whole other meaning to it, a special and life-changing meaning.

It's the day I chose myself. The day I chose to get the help I'd been surpressing for years. The day I chose self-love and care over feeling selfish. This was the start of a whole new journey for me. A journey I thought would be short and simple. Boy, was I wrong! But it was so worth it.

I'm very grateful for the journey I've endured.

The good, the enlightening, the horrifying, the hideous—I'm thankful for all the moments. If one moment didn't occur, the other wouldn't have followed. Everything works in a chain-reactive way, whether you think so or not.

Have you ever had a moment where you realized you never would have met someone or gotten a particular opportunity if this one person didn't know this other person you met through some event or another person? Or some odd connection like that? If you don't think so, really look back and think, was this truly all me, or was there a chain reaction before it got to me?

From a distance, people probably thought I was having the best year of my life. However, this has been one of the toughest years I've lived through. I'm honestly shocked I'm still here to write this piece today. I was in my darkest hole yet, only digging myself deeper. I made the most mistakes I've ever made in a year, but I'm grateful for every single one. I'm the woman I am today because of those mistakes. I'm stronger and wiser because of them.

I traveled a ton this past year, and I don't plan on stopping. Any cent I made, went to my next trip. Traveling invigorates me in ways I didn't know were possible. I learn so much from every trip I take. I meet incredible people in every location. I take risks my introverted self normally wouldn't back home. I feel free. I feel at peace with myself when I see more of this chaotic, beautiful world. I don't feel so much pressure in my chest about what the future holds. I feel more in the present, which is the only time we can control. I miss my friends and family with every trip, but they're always right where I left them when I come home. Traveling has helped my mental health in so many ways. I'm so grateful for the trips I've been able to experience so far.

I lost too many people this year, friendships, and relationships with many people. I've come to terms with most of the relationships lost, but there's those couple that'll sting every time you think of them. That's something I've grown to come to terms with better this past year as well—loss. The older I get, the older the ones I love get, too. I need to be confident in myself and know I will be okay when my support system trickles away from this world.

I've always struggled with loss. Never wanted to deal with it and its repercussions. I feel everything so deeply, so loss is something that hits my core even more. Again, this is something I've practiced coming to terms with better. Loss still hurts, but I need to understand that the world doesn't revolve around me and my losses. People lose someone every day. Who am I to think my loss is so much greater than those around me? Who am I to think my loss could hurt worse than my neighbors? I don't know the answers to these questions, but I now understand that the main subject in these questions is not supposed to be me.

I've also come to realize God takes people out of your life for a reason. We may not understand the reasons quite yet, but someday, we hopefully will. If we don't, then we can ask God himself someday why. At that point, I hope we understand that we don't always need to know the reason *why*. Sometimes, things just happen; sometimes, there isn't a miraculous reason we crave. That's something we will hopefully come to terms with and be okay.

In between trips, I was working and going to appointments. Some of these appointments included medication changes. "Medication changes" are now two words that make my skin crawl. I never knew how bad medication changes could be for your mental, emotional, and physical health until this past year.

Medication changes quite literally changed me without me knowing it until it was too late. It wasn't until after I had made a risky decision or purchase, said something I couldn't believe, and interrupted people when it's one of my biggest pet peeves that I have a recollection of "Wait, wtf was that?" I wasn't Karlee. I was wearing this mask of medication that made me a horrible, scary, untrustworthy person. I'm so glad I finally spoke up after two months of mania and absolute chaos that I was definitely not on the proper medication and was scared of myself at night.

After months of these changes, I changed too. I changed for the better. I rewired my brain and put it back on the "What was the point of this journey? You. Work on you" train. I'm not sure why self-care and love are so hard to work on for yourself, at least for someone like me. It's the most important kind of love. We cannot love and give away ourselves to others without having this love for ourselves, too. That's another thing I've learned.

I came into this journey thinking, "I want to be the absolute best version of myself, the best daughter, the best friend, the best girlfriend, the best wife someday, and overall, the best person I can be." That was my goal. This is a goal I won't meet until I'm six feet under. Why? Because all of these versions can always be worked on more. However, I've gotten a great start and realization of who I need to be, not only for myself but for everyone in my life.

One year ago today, I was terrified, numb, nervous, and empty. Today, I am full of the knowledge I learned in that unit. Today, I still get numb occasionally because nerves are something my anxiety still has control of, but I do not feel empty. I feel like my cup is filling. I'm not full; I'm not overflowing with glee and excitement yet. But I see something I didn't for so long… hope.

When you understand your power, you will understand that you always have a choice on what to focus on. You will make your own decisions, leave unhealthy relationships, and let go of everything holding you back. When you understand your power, you will become empowered. You will start taking responsibility for *every* aspect of your life. When you understand your power, you will also find what I found, and that is hope. May you always find hope.

-xoxo KayJo

APPENDIX

To anyone who has been to the hospital, I am so proud of you. To anyone negotiating whether they should go or not, give it a shot. The worst that can happen is you walk out with more information than when you walked in.

To anyone entering a hospital soon, here are some quotes and tips that immensely helped me throughout my stay and my journey afterward. Some of these are from the internet, some are from friends, and some I've found on my own, but most are from my great friend who struggles with similar issues that I do. I wrote some words of wisdom down before entering the hospital into my composition notebook I knew they wouldn't take. It became a companion during my growing journey, and I'm sharing that with you now.

LETTER OF HOPE

D*ear friend,*

No matter how down you're feeling, you likely always sidestep your feelings and care about everyone else's. It's what makes you brave, strong, and so impressive. I'm proud of you. You will never be able to please and/ or live up to some people's standards.

You are going to come out of this time in your life feeling different about things, and whatever those things are are valid, and so is your path. Going into this facility is about finding answers and working on you and your brain. Nothing else. It's not about anyone else or your situation even; it's just about you. Remember that.

You hold so much power. Even when it feels like you don't, you do. Your brain is your biggest enemy, and mastering it is a craft. You will master it.

Within uncertainty is potential. Within being lost is the chance to be found. Within discomfort is the space to allow change. Embrace it.

One day, you will look back on this time and see magic. Magic that you cared enough about you to get help. Magic that you had the strength to. Magic that you feel better than you did before. Magic that you had a support system and loved ones that never failed you.

Humans are amazing. From our darkest and most quiet hours, it's amazing how much we can change, learn, and grow. Believe that. Trust that. Know that you are one of those amazing humans and that you can be exactly who you dream to be. And that you will.

Sincerely,

A Very Dear Friend Who Understands

ENCOURAGING QUOTES

"Loneliness is the human condition. Cultivate it. The way it tunnels into you allows your soul room to grow. Never expect to outgrow loneliness. Never hope to find people who will understand you, someone to fill that space.

An intelligent, sensitive person is the exception, the very great exception. If you expect to find people who will understand you, you will grow murderous with disappointment. The best you'll ever do is to understand yourself, know what it is that you want, and not let the cattle stand in your way."

Janet Fitch, White Oleander

"Don't worry about what the world needs. Ask what makes you come alive and do that. Because what the world needs is people who have come alive."

Howard Thurman

"You can't stop the waves, but you can learn to surf."

Jon Kabat-Zinn

"You will hurt when you are meant to hurt. And love when you are meant to love. No matter how good you are to people, no matter what you do or don't do, whatever it may be—If it's meant for you, then it is meant for you. And it will show you what you need to know. What you need to experience in order for you to grow, and at the right time too.

Like I said, what is meant for you is meant for you, and no one can take that away. No one can dictate what is going on in your life right now at this very *instant. Just know [that] how it is, [is] exactly where you need to be. So, take these experiences as they come. Take them in with all [your] heart.*

With all [your] soul. And at your own pace. There are lessons to be learned from everything. Bad or good. Lessons to be passed down, despite your best efforts to avoid them."

R.M. Drake

"I will not apologize for choosing myself this time. Self-love is the chapter that I've always wanted to write."

S.R.W

"And once the storm is over, you won't remember how you made it through, how you managed to survive. You won't even be sure whether the storm is really over. But one thing is certain: when you come out of the storm, you won't be the same person who walked in."

Haruki Murakami

"Don't judge my choices when you don't understand my reasons."

The Joker

"But the Lord stood with me and gave me strength."

2 Timothy 4:17

"I will praise thee; for I am fearfully and wonderfully made: marvelous are thy works; and that my soul knoweth right well."

Psalm 139:14

"Return to yourself: sometimes it takes losing yourself many times before you understand that you need yourself more than you need anyone else."

"Expectations are the root of heartache."

"Know that the pain will pass, and when it passes, you will become stronger, happier, more sensitive and aware."

"Having anxiety and depression is like being scared and tired at the same time. It's the fear of failure, but [with] no urge to be productive. It's wanting friends but hate socializing. It's wanting to be alone but not wanting to be lonely. It's feeling everything at once, then feeling paralyzingly numb."

"At some point, you have to realize that some people can stay in your heart but not in your life."

"A single moment of misunderstanding is so poisonous that it makes us forget the hundred lovable moments spent together within a minute."

"I think part of the reason why we hold on to something so tight is that we fear something so great won't happen twice."

"The days that break you are the days that make you."

SOME OF THE MOST COMMON THINKING DISTORTIONS WE USE:

1. **Mind Reading**: Using our perception of body language or past experiences to believe we know what someone is thinking.

Example: A friend of mine passes me on the street and does not say hello. I begin to think, "He is just ignoring me. He does not like me anymore."

2. **Catastrophizing:** Making negative predictions about the future based on little or no evidence.

3. **All-or-Nothing-Thinking:** "All or Nothing" thinker sees things as all black or all white, but never gray.

Example: "If I do not do something perfect, then I am a complete failure," or "If my significant other breaks up with me, I will never find another person."

4. **Emotional Reasoning:** Assuming that because we feel a certain way, it must be true.

Example: "I feel overwhelmed and hopeless. It means that my problems are so big that they are impossible to solve. There is no hope for me."

5. **Labeling:** Giving yourself or others a single negative label.

Example: "I am so stupid" after staying in a dysfunctional relationship or "He is such a loser" for not completing a college degree.

6. **Mental Filtering**: Focusing on the negative aspects of a situation and ignoring the positive ones. Mental filtering fails to take into consideration the whole of a person's experience, which often includes things that are both positive and negative.

Example: "My boss gave me positive feedback on my yearly review, but one negative comment and all I can think about is the one comment that was negative."

7. **Overgeneralization:** The distortion differs due to a tendency to perceive a global pattern of negatives on the basis of a single incident. Draws a conclusion about an entire group, topic, or place based upon insufficient evidence.

Example: "I had a negative experience in one relationship; I am not good in any relationship."

8. **Personalization:** Blaming yourself, or someone else, for a situation that, in reality, involved many factors that were out of your control.

Example: "If I had stayed with my wife that night, she wouldn't have driven home drunk and wrecked her car." Or "If I would have lost more weight, my boyfriend wouldn't have cheated on me."

9. **Should Statements:** Believing that certain things "should" or "must" be true. Assuming there is some all-encompassing law or rule that something must be true or should happen.

Example: "I should be able to fight my mental health illness on my own," or "I should be better by now."

10. **Discounting the Positives:** Looking at our past positive accomplishments or qualities and finding reasons why they are false.

Example: Your friend tells you she loves you and you are beautiful, but your thought is, "She is just saying that because she is my friend."

11. **Fortune-Telling:** Predicting the future and believing you can know how a situation will end.

Example: "I am going to go home after being at Avera and will do well for a couple days, but then I will be back here within a week because my skills won't work." Or "My cholesterol is going to be sky-high."

12. **Comparison:** Interpret events in terms of unrealistic standards. Mainly focus on others who do better than you and find yourself less than in comparison.

Example: "The neighbor kid can already read in kindergarten, and my child is just learning the alphabet. I'm a bad parent."

13. **Blaming:** Blaming occurs when you focus on the other person as the *source* of your negative feelings and you refuse to take responsibility for changing yourself.

Example: "I was driving 10 miles over the speed limit when I was pulled over by a police officer who parked in a non-visible area on the road. I blamed the officer for setting a trap."

14. **Magnification:** Blowing a situation out of proportion to reality. Making a mountain out of a molehill.

 Example: "A car pulled out in front of me on the way to work. He was trying to make me late for work and ruin my whole day!"

15. **Minimization:** Taking a big situation and making light of it.

 Example: "I got an award at church but it isn't a big deal as other people have received the reward as well."

GROUNDING

Whenever you feel like you have lost control of yourself or your surroundings, ground yourself. Usually, you'll get the best results when you ground yourself outside. Take off your shoes, and get your toes in the grass or sand or even snow if you want.

First, take some deep breaths, and continue taking deep breaths during your entire grounding routine. Then you're going to find:

5 things you can *see*

4 things you can *touch*

3 things you can *hear*

2 things you can *smell*

1 thing you can *taste*

All of your senses will *always* be waiting for you to use them so you can experience the most you can out of this life.

Grounding is something I do often. In fact, I do it daily now without even realizing it sometimes. Whenever I feel anxious or overwhelmed with my life, myself, or this world, I ground myself. After grounding, I constantly feel better, even if it is just a teeny tiny bit.

SOME THINGS THAT HELP DEPRESSION

1. Being kind to yourself

2. Taking a bath

3. Moving your body

4. Writing or drawing

5. Calming music

6. Cleaning your space

7. Crying

8. Talking to a friend

9. Reading a book

10. Exercise

11. Asking for help

12. Going to therapy

13. Making a Happy Jar

14. Find a routine

15. Organizing

16. Playing a musical instrument

17. Hydration

18. Rest

19. Giving yourself grace

99 Positive Coping Skills

1. Exercise

2. Put on fake tattoos (or be like me and get real ones)

3. Write (poetry, stories, journal)

4. Scribble/doodle on paper

5. Be with other people

6. Watch a favorite TV show

7. Hydrate

8. Go see a movie

9. Do a word search or crossword

10. Do schoolwork

11. Play a musical instrument

12. Paint your nails, do your make-up or hair

13. Sing

14. Study the sky

15. Punch a pillow

16. Cover yourself with Band-Aids where you want to cut

17. Let yourself cry

18. Take a nap (only if you are tired)

19. Take a hot shower or relaxing bath

20. Play with a pet

21. Go shopping

22. Clean something

23. Knit or sew

24. Read a good book

25. Listen to some music

26. Try some aromatherapy (candle, lotion, room spray, oils)

27. Meditate

28. Go somewhere very public

29. Bake cookies

30. Create a vision board

31. Paint or draw

32. Rip paper into itty bitty pieces.

33. Shoot hoops, kick a ball.

34. Write a letter or send an email

35. Plan your dream room (colors/furniture)

36. Hug a pillow or stuffed animal

37. Hyper-focus on something like a rock, hand, etc.

38. Dance

39. Make hot chocolate, a milkshake, or a smoothie

40. Play with modeling clay or Play-Doh

41. Build a pillow fort

42. Go for a nice long drive

43. Complete something you've been putting off

44. Draw on yourself with a marker

45. Take up a new hobby

46. Look up recipes, cook a meal

47. Go outside for 15 minutes

48. Create or build something

49. Pray

50. Make a list of blessings in your life

51. Read the Bible

52. Go to a friend's house

53. Jump on a trampoline

54. Watch an old, happy movie

55. Contact a hotline/your therapist (If you want to call us, 1-800-448-3000)

56. Talk to someone close to you

57. Ride a bicycle

58. Feed the ducks, birds, or squirrels

59. Color

60. Memorize a poem, play, or song

61. Stretch

62. Search for ridiculous things on the internet

63. "Shop" online (without buying anything)

64. Color coordinate your wardrobe

65. Watch fish

66. Make a playlist of your favorite songs.

67. Play the "15 Minute Game" (Avoid something for 15 minutes, when time is up, start again)

68. Plan your wedding/prom/other event

69. Plant some seeds

70. Hunt for your perfect home or car online

71. Try to make as many words out of your full name as possible

72. Sort through/edit your pictures

73. Play with a balloon

74. Give yourself a facial

75. Play with a favorite childhood toy

76. Start collecting something

77. Play a video/computer game

78. Clean up trash at your local park

79. Watch some funny Tik-Toks

80. Text or call a friend

81. Write yourself an "I love you because…" letter

82. Look up new words and use them

83. Rearrange furniture

84. Write a letter to someone that you may never send

85. Smile at five people

86. Play with your little sister/brother/niece/nephew

87. Go for a walk (with or without a friend)

88. Put a puzzle together

89. Clean your room/closet

90. Try to do handstands, cartwheels, or backbends

91. Yoga

92. Teach your pet a new trick

93. Learn a new language

94. Move everything in your room to a new spot

95. Get together with friends to play frisbee, soccer, or basketball

96. Hug a friend or family member

97. Search online for new songs/artists.

98. Make a list of goals for the week/month/year/5 years

99. Perform a random act of kindness

Affirmations

Affirmations are positive statements that you can speak out loud or silently. They will impact your life in ways you never thought were possible. Positive affirmations do work if they are practiced daily and correctly.

102 Positive Affirmations

1. I am successful in whatever I do.

2. I plan my work and work my plan.

3. I will focus on what is truly essential.

4. I will make the most of new opportunities.

5. Good flows to me; good flows from me.

6. I feel wonderful and alive.

7. I feel the joy of abundance.

8. I speak with confidence and calm assurance.

9. The universe provides for my every want and need.

10. I am healthy and happy.

11. I have a lot of energy.

12. I radiate happiness.

13. Everything is getting better every day.

14. My mind is calm.

15. I am always on the path to success and victory.

16. I am at peace with myself.

17. I find peace and joy in all aspects of my life.

18. I have value, and I matter.

19. I am happy.

20. I feel joy, love, and abundance.

21. I am one with my inner child.

22. I am amazing.

23. I can do anything.

24. I am prepared to succeed.

25. Positivity is a choice.

26. I am fabulous, funny, and giving.

27. I am outstanding.

28. I am unique and special, and most importantly, I am me.

29. I am financially free.

30. I am perfect, exactly as I am.

31. I focus on what is truly essential.

32. I make positive, healthy choices.

33. I am in control of my reactions.

34. I find all solutions within me.

35.   All is well in my life.

36.   I will make the most of new opportunities.

37.   I organize my priorities with clarity.

38.   I forgive myself.

39.   I am forgiven.

40.   I will always be there for myself.

41.   I enjoy the variety of life.

42.   I am my own guru.

43.   I take good care of myself.

44.   I am patient with myself.

45.   I let go of my past.

46.   I am evolving eternally.

47.   I know I can always upgrade.

48.   There is a gift for me in everything that I experience.

49.   I follow my inner guidance.

50.   I appreciate my physical body.

51.   I treat my body well.

52.   I take it easy.

53.   I make room for fun and playfulness.

54.   I appreciate intimacy.

55.   I am very good at letting go.

56.   I am grateful for my life.

57.   I love being myself.

58.   Time is on my side.

59.   I surrender to love.

60.   I invite bliss.

61.   I learn from the past.

62.   I am good at walking the talk.

63.   I enjoy being taken good care of by the universe.

64.   I create my reality on a continuous basis.

65.   My body is healthy.

66.   I am superior to negative thoughts and low actions.

67.   I forgive those who have harmed me in my past and peacefully detach myself from them.

68.   I possess the qualities needed to be extremely successful.

69.   My business is growing, expanding, and thriving.

70.   My ability to conquer my challenges is limitless.

71.   My potential to succeed is infinite.

72.   I am courageous, and I stand up for myself.

73.   My thoughts are filled with positivity, and my life is filled with prosperity.

74.   I am blessed with an incredible family and wonderful friends.

75.   I am a powerhouse.

76.   My future is an ideal projection of what I envision now.

77. I radiate beauty, charm, and grace. I am conquering my illness.

78. I wake up today with strength in my heart and clarity in my mind.

79. My fears of tomorrow are simply melting away.

80. My life is just beginning.

81. The assertion that something exists or is true.

82. I always have everything I need to be happy.

83. I live a positive life and only attract the best in my life.

84. I am peacefully allowing my life to unfold.

85. Today and every day, I choose to be happy.

86. I am fun energetic, and people love me for it.

87. My life overflows with happiness and love.

88. Today is rich with opportunities, and I open my heart to receive them.

89. I take the time to show my friends that I care about them.

90. I am thankful that I get to live another day.

91. I see the world with beauty and color.

92. I deserve whatever good comes my way today.

93. I believe in myself.

94. I radiate confidence, certainty, and optimism.

95. I courageously open and move through every door of opportunity.

96. I am in charge of my life.

97. I have the power to love my dreams.

98. My mind has unlimited power.

99. I stand up for what I believe in.

100. I act with courage and confidence.

101. I love myself more every day.

102. I am blessed with an incredible family and wonderful friends.

More of My Favorite Quotes

"One day, you will wake up, and all of a sudden, the weight of the last few weeks, months, or even years will be lifted off your shoulders. You can't control when that day comes; all you can do is stay strong and trust that it is coming."

"Sometimes you have to forget what you feel and remember what you deserve."

"I'm not in this universe to live up to your expectations, and you are not in this universe to live up to mine."

"Sometimes God is going to give you the same test over and over until you know better because to know better is to do better. God places us on a journey of repeated tests, not to break us, but to form us into our best selves."

"You're gonna be happy," said life, "but first, I'll make you strong."

"I am learning to love the sound of my feet walking away from things that aren't meant for me."

"I hope you believe that you can still make a beautiful life for yourself even if you lost many years of it to grief, or darkness, or a wound that wouldn't close."

"There is nothing impossible to they who will try."

Alexander The Great

"A person is but the product of their thoughts. What they think, they become."

Mahatma Gandhi

"Life begins at the end of your comfort zone."

Neale Donald Walsch

"Do not spoil what you have by desiring what you have not; remember that what you now have was once among the things you only hoped for."

Epicurus

"Anyone who has actually been that sad can tell you that there's nothing beautiful or literary or mysterious about depression."

Jasmine Warga

"If you know someone's depressed, please resolve never to ask them why. Depression isn't a straightforward response to a bad situation. Depression just is, like the weather."

Stephen Fry

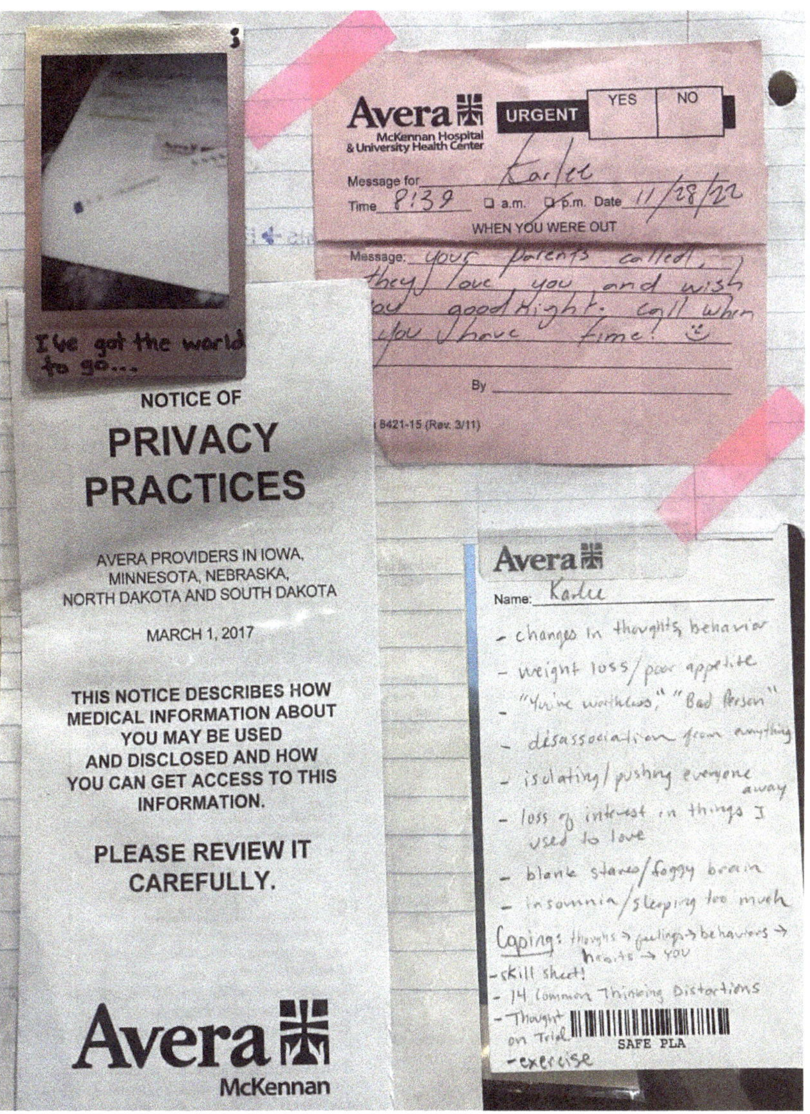
I've got the world
to go...

Avera
McKennan Hospital
& University Health Center
URGENT   YES   NO
Message for   Karlee
Time   8:39   a.m.   p.m.   Date   11/28/22
WHEN YOU WERE OUT
Message: your parents called,
they love you and wish
you good night. call when
you have time!
By
8421-15 (Rev. 3/11)

NOTICE OF
PRIVACY
PRACTICES

AVERA PROVIDERS IN IOWA,
MINNESOTA, NEBRASKA,
NORTH DAKOTA AND SOUTH DAKOTA

MARCH 1, 2017

THIS NOTICE DESCRIBES HOW
MEDICAL INFORMATION ABOUT
YOU MAY BE USED
AND DISCLOSED AND HOW
YOU CAN GET ACCESS TO THIS
INFORMATION.

PLEASE REVIEW IT
CAREFULLY.

Avera
McKennan

Avera
Name: Karlee
- changes in thoughts & behavior
- weight loss / poor appetite
- "You're worthless," "Bad Person"
- disassociation from anything
- isolating / pushing everyone away
- loss of interest in things I used to love
- blank stares / foggy brain
- insomnia / sleeping too much
Coping: thoughts → feelings → behaviors → habits → you
- skill sheet!
- 14 Common Thinking Distortions
- Thought on Trial
SAFE PLA
- exercise

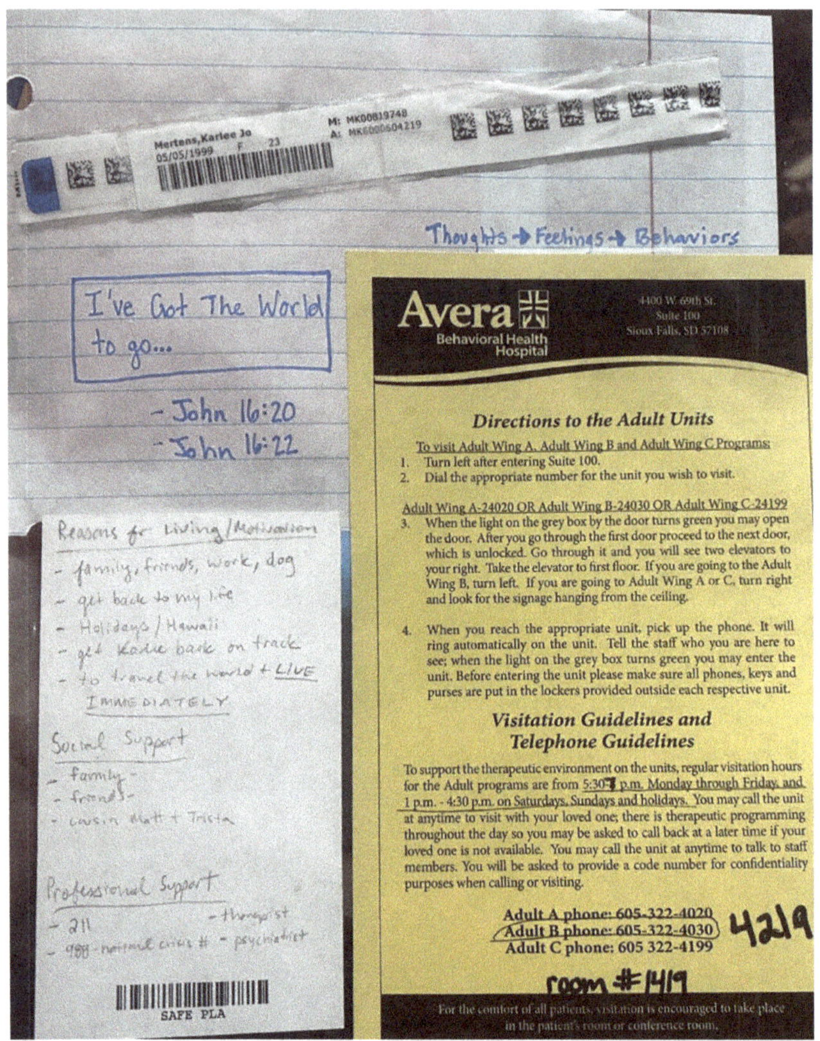
Thoughts → Feelings → Behaviors

I've Got The World to go...

- John 16:20
- John 16:22

Reasons for Living / Motivation
- family, friends, work, dog
- get back to my life
- Holidays / Hawaii
- get Katie back on track
- to travel the world + LIVE IMMEDIATELY

Social Support
- family -
- friends -
- cousins Matt + Trista

Professional Support
- 211   - therapist
- 988 - national crisis # - psychiatrist

SAFE PLA

Mertens, Karlee Jo
05/05/1999   F   23
M: MK00819748
A: MK6000604219

Avera
Behavioral Health
Hospital

4400 W. 69th St.
Suite 100
Sioux Falls, SD 57108

Directions to the Adult Units

To visit Adult Wing A, Adult Wing B and Adult Wing C Programs:
1. Turn left after entering Suite 100.
2. Dial the appropriate number for the unit you wish to visit.

Adult Wing A-24020 OR Adult Wing B-24030 OR Adult Wing C-24199
3. When the light on the grey box by the door turns green you may open the door. After you go through the first door proceed to the next door, which is unlocked. Go through it and you will see two elevators to your right. Take the elevator to first floor. If you are going to the Adult Wing B, turn left. If you are going to Adult Wing A or C, turn right and look for the signage hanging from the ceiling.

4. When you reach the appropriate unit, pick up the phone. It will ring automatically on the unit. Tell the staff who you are here to see; when the light on the grey box turns green you may enter the unit. Before entering the unit please make sure all phones, keys and purses are put in the lockers provided outside each respective unit.

Visitation Guidelines and
Telephone Guidelines

To support the therapeutic environment on the units, regular visitation hours for the Adult programs are from 5:30 p.m. Monday through Friday, and 1 p.m. - 4:30 p.m. on Saturdays, Sundays and holidays. You may call the unit at anytime to visit with your loved one; there is therapeutic programming throughout the day so you may be asked to call back at a later time if your loved one is not available. You may call the unit at anytime to talk to staff members. You will be asked to provide a code number for confidentiality purposes when calling or visiting.

Adult A phone: 605-322-4020
Adult B phone: 605-322-4030
Adult C phone: 605 322-4199

4219

room # 1419

For the comfort of all patients, visitation is encouraged to take place
in the patient's room or conference room,

ACKNOWLEDGMENTS

There are many people I have to thank who have supported me throughout my journey, whether during my hospital stay or in the chapter before or after it. I am immensely grateful for their care and presence in my life. With all my heart, thank you.

First, a special thank you to my counselor, Angie Arnold, for being the best counselor I could ask for since the age of sixteen. She knows all the nitty gritty details about me and my life and still supports me constantly.

Not just because it's her job but because she genuinely cares. Week after week, she makes me feel better. I want to thank her for encouraging me to go to the unit in the first place. She also encouraged me to write about my experiences while being in the unit. I would not have this book without her. After reading my journal to her, she told me to make it into a book. I also want to thank you for always being there when I need you. No matter what time or day, you're there to help me, even when you're away from the office. Your words of wisdom have helped and saved me many nights. Thank you so much, Angie.

I'm grateful to Avera McKennan Behavioral Unit and all the doctors, psychiatrists, nurses, and staff there.

Thank you for doing what you do. Thank you for having this program available. Thank you for all the patience, hard work, long hours, care, and support you all showed, not only for myself but for every patient at that hospital. I thank you for giving me the tools that allowed me to save my life. Words will never be enough. Thank you.

Thank you to my psychiatrist, Brenda Johnson. Thank you for finding the scientific formula for my brain.

Thank you for the trials and tribulations throughout my medication journey and for calmly taking care of every version of me. Thank you for all your support and patience with me. Medication changes are not easy, and you get the brunt of how I'm feeling sometimes. I appreciate your amazing brain and the effort you put into trying to figure out mine. Thank you from the bottom of my heart. It's hard to imagine where I'd be if I never met you and hadn't started this journey together.

I'm grateful for Dr. Ethan Helder. Thank you for your medical expertise in healing my stomach issues. I also want to thank Dr. Helder for introducing me to the acupuncture world and its phenomenal results. After nearly a decade of issues, his holistic approach cured my guts and has immensely changed my life. Thank you, Dr. Helder.

Kristine Skiff, thank you for helping me in the process of publishing my first book. You were so clear and concise about the process of things and made this experience so much easier. Thank you for always being there whenever I had questions. Thank you for being so open and honest with me about my book. Thank you for helping me find the right editor and instigating that process. I was so worried about finding the right publisher for my first book, and you made it seem so simple and fun.

I'm so grateful to my parents, Darin and Lesa Mertens. I cannot thank you both enough for being the best set of parents I could ask for. Thank you for taking me to all of the doctor appointments and for taking me there at all. I am so grateful to be in a family with not only excellent emotional support but also financial support as well. I am more than fortunate to have been able to go to the hospital in the first place. Thank you for always encouraging me to chase my dreams and let my wings soar.

Mom, first off, thank you for bringing me into this world. Thank you for taking the time to teach me "woman" things like how to cook, bake, sew, etc. Not to mention all the life lessons you've taught me in my 24 years on this earth. I never realized how true the statement of mothers feeling what their children feel, but sometimes harder, until having my mental health issues. It's quite damaging what depression, mania, insomnia, anxiety, and all my issues can do to our relationship. Just one of these issues would be hard to deal with, but you get to deal with a daughter who has a full resume. It's completely and totally heartbreaking.

Every time I go through an episode, you do, too. I can't imagine the amount of worry and angst I put you through. I always think how hard it must be to be my parent. I thank you for loving the hell out of me. I thank you for always looking into new treatments, ideas, and products to help my depression and issues. I appreciate your effort and care more than you know. Even when it seems I'm annoyed. I look up to you in so many ways and am so grateful for you and your love. I aspire to be half the woman you are someday with an ounce of that patience. I love you so much, Mama.

Dad, thank you for being the best dad I could ask for. I can't imagine the way I'd have turned out without a dad like you. Thank you for all of the amazing lifelong lessons you've taught me. You never got your son, but you got three girls who will hunt with you. I'm so grateful for you teaching me how to hunt and pushing me year after year in the field. I also appreciate all your fun facts about life that are very handy for any type of situation. I want to apologize whenever I am a certain way and you just can't wrap your mind around it.

You've tried to understand for so many years. You've gone out of your way to learn certain words and their definitions to understand better. The misunderstanding in your eyes kills me, as I wish that I had understood it and could have explained it all better. I appreciate your desire to learn and understand better. That means more than you'd ever know. Thank you for always being my rock. One of my favorite squeezes to receive. Being a daddy's girl, I've grown to tell you just about anything. I'm so grateful for how close we are and for our relationship. Many sons and daughters will never receive an ounce of the love I've received from you. I love you so much, Padre.

To my two sisters, McKenzie and Lindsey, I thank you for the endless years of support and love. You two have been the ones to get me through my dark times when I was unmedicated and unsure of what issues I even had. You guys love me incredibly, if not more, due to the issues I contain. You both have your own unique ways of helping me through my lulls and dark times. Both of you have been perfectly chosen to be sisters to such a hot mess. You handle me so well. Most of the time.

To my family, thank you for your patience and kind hearts towards me. Your support is something I'll eternally be grateful for. I'm still unsure as to how and why I have the most supportive support system out there. I'm incredibly blessed to have the same blood as you all. Thank you so much for your continual care, love, and support.

To my boss, Dr. Jessi Warrington, and my coworkers, thank you for your patience and words of encouragement throughout this journey. Dr. Jessi, if it wasn't for our relationship and communication, I wouldn't be where I am today. If I never sat down and had one of the most challenging conversations I've ever had after you pulled me aside, my story wouldn't be where it is today. I have a lot of people to thank on this journey. Still, that conversation, that start to this journey of, "Hey, it's time you get some more help for the betterment of not only your work self but, most importantly, your overall self," really sticks out to me in my thank you category. Those were words I needed to hear from anyone, let alone someone I look up to and respect so highly. That vulnerable conversation left me with validation of what my next steps were. Sometimes, a little validation is all you need. After that conversation, I was in contact with my counselor and in the hospital a week later. I remember leaving the clinic bawling as I felt like I had lost the job of my dreams like my depression ripped away yet another thing I loved.

When in reality, I was given enough grace to be put on leave, not fired. I was given a second chance at not only work but my life. Words cannot thank you enough, Dr. Jessi. As time went on, you guys never forgot about me. Many workplaces wouldn't work with me on leave. They'd simply fire me. Not this group, though; they have stuck with me this entire year. They never stopped checking in, inviting me to work dinners and work occasions. I miss my boss, coworkers, and clients so much. Not to mention all the small and big fur babies I was fortunate enough to work with daily. It's an agonizing pain to be taken away from something you love, especially when it's 'all about you.' It's been a long, strenuous year away from my home away from home, but your animal lover couldn't stay away. I'm so happy and excited to say I'm finally back working at the clinic as of December 9th, 2023.

My partner, my firecracker, my rock, my hard-working, energetic, optimistic, and happy-go-lucky teddy bear, thank you for absolutely everything. From our first memory to our last meet-up to exchange Nali, thank you. You've filled my heart and mind with so many blissful, amazing memories that no one can ever take away. I'll cherish them forever. Thank you for loving me to the fullest, the hardest, with the best love I've ever received. Thank you for your understanding during this confusing time. You respected my space and time better than most could. You're so incredibly strong. I'm so proud of you for so many reasons. Being in the opposite seat this year, I've come to realize just how incredibly strong and patient you are. It's made me love you more. I want to thank you for all our memories, good and bad. You are truly a gift to this world, and I'm extremely blessed to have been loved by you. To have known you. One of my favorite quotes I think about often if things never mend is: *And even if you aren't here to stay, I'm glad the universe allowed your soul to stop by.* You will forever be my favorite person, my best friend, the one who showed me true love. You were and still are my favorite chapter. I can look at it and smile at it. Thank you, Brett. I miss and adore you and will forever love you.

Thank you to my partner's amazing family. Thank you for your patience, love, and support. Thank you for understanding this process and still showering me with love over the amount of time I've taken. I apologize for the time I've taken, but it was necessary. I appreciate all of the help you've shown Brett, Nali, and me.

Without you guys, it's hard to picture how life could have been the past 4 years. I know it would have been very dull without your support. Your family has loved and cared for me in ways I've only dreamed of as a potential mother and father-in-law. The both of you consistently made sure my belly was full, and my head wasn't aching. I'll never be able to thank you enough, but here is a written thank you. I miss and love you guys dearly.

Morgan Smith, thank you for being like another dad or uncle in my life. For as long as I can remember, you have been in my family's life. I am so grateful to not only know you and hunt with you but also to be able to receive the fantastic advice you give. You are an inspiration to me, and I hope I can be as kind, driven, and successful someday. I'd also like to thank you for any and all financial support you have either given or loaned me. I can never thank you enough. You are the entrepreneurial superstar I look up to. I aspire to be a version of you someday, but the woman-badass version, of course. I appreciate all the love and support you've shown me and my family for the entirety of my life. Thank you, and I love you, Morgan Smith.

Jake Youngblood Dobbs, thank you for starting an incredible online community and allowing me to be a part of it. I now consider this community as less of a community and more of a family. We support each other in whatever endeavors we are pursuing. While showering each other with love and advice. It's an incredible feeling having strangers across the world rooting and cheering you on. It wasn't until this community that I truly realized how amazing the coming of different minds with different opinions, ethnicities, and backgrounds is. I have found purpose through this family. Thank you, Jake. You've created something absolutely beautiful. I'll never be able to thank you enough for creating something that quite literally 360'd my life around. You are so appreciated. I am entirely grateful to have you in my life; thank you.

Thank you to my friends who supported me and still loved me throughout this hectic rollercoaster. Thank you for sticking with me alongside my journey. You know who you are. Thank you so much. I'll never be able to put into words how much that means, and it will forever mean to me.

The following shoutouts to these friends who have my utmost thanks:

Trevor Blaszczyk, my optimistic fireball, thank you for continuing to support and encourage me. We met through an online group called Irrational Optimists.

Now, it seems impossible to not have him in my life. He has had me on his podcast, 'Mind Over Matter,' twice to talk about mental health. We have grown especially close bonding over our care and love for other humans in the world who are without mental healthcare, along with those with any mental health issues at all. He was also my knight in shining armor, and he saved me from a disastrous trip where I was stranded alone in Miami.

He drove 4 hours, had his car break down, and rented a new car, all within 7 hours. All to come and make sure I wasn't staying alone in Miami. We had the most spontaneous trip of a lifetime with no plan. He has also immensely helped me with the editing and publishing part of my book, as well as helping me create my first website and creating merchandise to sell. He is, without a doubt, there when I need him. The way he views the world is something I wish I could do more of. He has an insanely positive, realistic, and resilient perspective on this life. He is the definition of a brilliant, amazing, and a blessing of a person to have in your life. The type you want to keep around forever. Thank you, Trev.

Paige DeVries, my motivated, determined, and most hilarious best friend, thank you for your support and love from the moment we met during my freshman year of college. When we first met, we clicked and have consistently been each other's rocks. We've shared so many amazing memories, traveled, and been through hell and back together. We have both saved each other at one point or another during our time as friends. I'll never forget the one night I almost overdosed, but you, PD, knocked on my door and came in and talked me out of it. You've also saved me this past year with your genuine friendship. A friendship I didn't need to worry about losing. A solid human I could always count on whenever, wherever, and in whatever situation.

Thank you for letting me stay with you twice at your home in Colorado while showing me some of Colorado's beauty. Those are times I'll never forget.

When all I saw was black, grey, and white, you let me escape with you to see these new vivid watercolors. Times when I saw hope, peace, and happiness again. Those are life-changing moments for which I can't thank you enough. Your hard-working self is something I'll forever admire about you. You, Miss Paige DeVries, can and WILL go anywhere. Thank you for sticking with me on my journey and never giving up on me. I thank and love you so much, PD.

Rachel Speck, my twin flame, thank you for your support, love, perspective on life, and overall for being the person you are. You were a Godsent friend that appeared at the most crucial time in my life. It's crazy to think how we met and how close we got so fast. It's hard to imagine I didn't have you in my life for the first twenty-one and a half years. You have changed my mindset and the way I see things and the world. Thank you for helping me plan my first solo trip to come and see you in Hawaii. Thank you also for letting me stay with you and the amazing Lexi Fredrichs. Thank you for showing me paradise while saying this is your home. You were the person who showed me something that made happy tears fall. That's a moment I'll never forget; feeling serenity, peace, and such inner happiness the first 10 seconds outside in the Hawaiian air that I just cried. For the first time in months, I felt alive and at peace again. You supplied the toolkit for this. I'll never be able to thank you enough for all of the Facetimes and words of wisdom before and after the hospital. I use and share so many of the quotes you sent me, as well as the ones you create with your own mind with others. I genuinely don't know where I'd be without you in my life. I'm so entirely grateful for our relationship. God truly blessed me with you. I adore the memories made and cannot wait for more memories to come.

Thank you, I love you, Rachel, babes.

QUAD, my best friends since Pre-K, and my First and Third Grade for the other two. All the way through puberty and middle school, to football games and High School, to all being split up for college, and all remaining friends in the meantime –thank you. The three of us reside together in our hometown. Two are not planning on going anywhere anytime soon as they have husbands, and each has a kid of their own. We've remained friends throughout many different, challenging, life-changing events. This is a group of gals I'm sure will be in my life forever. As we've grown, they've watched me grow and develop new illnesses as time has gone on. Never once did I feel like I was a burden to them. They never made me feel odd for talking about my issues or not wanting to talk at all. These three gals have been there for everything. They could each write a book about me if they were told to, as I could for them. I love these girls and all their years of support. I genuinely don't know what I did to deserve such a great group of sisters.

Clare Folk, my very first friend, and my first best friend, thank you for sticking with me since Pre-K. From our first fight over an electronic piano in Pre-K to our latest wine night, you've seen it all. You've seen the absolute worst of the worst and best of the best moments.

You've been there and supported me through it all. You never left my side. You've witnessed me grow into the woman I am today. All the good, bad, and the ugly, you never thought to ditch me. You've always been my friend who instills my faith in me and often reminds me of the Lord and his ways. You've always been the one praying for me, rooting for me, and that's something I can't thank you enough for. You've always been the caretaker, the mom, the one who you can tell absolutely anything without a doubt it'll leave your mouth. Thank you for your decades of support and love. You're stuck with me for life. Thank you, ClareBear, I love you so much.

Madison Bowsher, my naturally hilarious best friend, thank you for being so amazingly supportive and understanding since we met in Third Grade. You've never left my side. You were always the friend who knew when I was going through something and told me I could always talk to you. We understand each other on a deeper level with the issues we share. We definitely had our share of talks, but there were too many to count. If only we had microphones and a camera, we could have had a fantastic podcast. You've always been the friend I never needed to explain my emotions to. You just knew and understood. Your kind, caring eyes are something I'll always be able to pour my heart out to. You have one of the kindest, most tender hearts I've met in this life. I'm so grateful for all of the unforgettable memories we've made so far and I cheer at the thought of those to come. I love you, Mads, thank you.

Macie Redmond, my little ray of sunshine, my voice of reason, thank you for sticking alongside me since we met in Third Grade. Our relationship has only grown year after year. Thank you for being so supportive and kind to me from the start. You've always said you didn't quite understand depression, but you'd do anything to take it away from me. I'm not sure if you understood how much you'd be taking on, but that phrase alone beautifully reflects your character. Thank you for letting me rant and never making me feel crazy. Your support, kind words, and love are things I've never taken for granted and never will. Cheers to the many memories to come! I love you, Mace, thank you.

Taya Bauer, my Taurus twin, thank you for being the friend I needed my whole life over the past three years. It's crazy how life works and when God chooses to place certain people in your life. Your words of encouragement, accountability checks, talks about therapy, your dark humor, and overall, your personality have gotten me through multiple bad days and nights. I'll never forget the amount of support you showed me and my family when I told you I was checking myself in.

I'll forever be grateful to *The Brewhouse* for meeting the best barista there ever was and having our friendship grow from there. From coffee dates to your wedding, to random wine nights in the middle, I appreciate every single memory with you. You are a forever type of friend that no one wants to lose. I'm so entirely grateful for you and our friendship. Thank you for joining me on my journey and sticking with me when things got tough. I love you and thank you, Taya, babes.

Clarissa Blake, my optimistic cheerleader, thank you for your support and love. You have been someone who has always been there for me. I can never thank a friend enough for sticking around, supporting, and loving me enough. Mere words could never do my feelings justice. I also want to thank you for helping me with the editing portion of my book. Thank you for listening to me read countless chapters and portions of my book and for your genuine advice afterward. You are such a light to this world, and bring it with you everywhere you go.

You are one of the strongest warriors I know, and I am grateful to know you, let alone know you the way I do. I'm so thankful God placed you in my life for so many years. You will always be a friend

I can count on, and that's an incredible compliment to have. Thank you for sticking alongside me and my journey. I love you, Clar.

Alyssa Haaland, my bubbly ray of sunshine, thank you for sticking with me alongside my journey, both life and mental health-related. You've always been that friend that I can talk to without a doubt about what's going on in my head. You never judged me, only showered me with light, positivity, and words of encouragement. I'll never be able to thank you enough for all the support and love you've shown me since the moment we met during my freshman year of college. Speaking of that night, you already know how much you saved me during that time in my life. If it wasn't for you, my path would have ended up so differently. You saved me multiple more times since then. These are merely things that cannot be thanked enough for through words. I cherish every memory from that first beach party, every coffee and errand date, randomly entertaining ourselves at home, to our last porch party at 1808. Not to mention our latest vintage/thrift binge-shopping days. Thank you for sticking with me, Lyss. I love you so much.

Erica Ulberg, thank you for continuing to be one of the few constants I have in this life. You've been someone I've looked up to in many ways ever since we met. Our friendship was one that blossomed at a time when I needed a role model. I was a little Freshman, and you had just moved to town for your Senior year. I remember thinking how cool it felt to be able to hang out with the new, super-talented, and pretty Senior. Our personalities just meshed perfectly. The age gap wasn't a thing we ever thought of. After you graduated, you continued to consistently show your love year after year. Thank you for always being that friend I can count on, no matter where this crazy life takes you. Finally, you have moved home, and I couldn't be more excited for the memories to come. Thank you, Erica. You've shown me so much in this life, and I cannot wait for what's next. I love you.

Lucien Sebert, thank you for continuously encouraging me to write it out, to get it out, and overall, to go for it. You've consistently been that friend who pushes others around you to just do it. Your energy goes a long way. Your words of wisdom have never gone unheard. I thank you for all our talks about life and our philosophy of it all. Thank you for also encouraging me to join 'Irrational Optimists,' the group that immensely changed my mindset and perspective on people and the world. This group helped me find my true purpose.

Every time I wanted to quit and not finish the book, I kept thinking, what would Bert do. Thank you for the countless memories that I'll forever cherish. Thank you, Bert.

My person at one time, thank you for your years of support. When we first met, it felt like I met the love of my life in girl form. We connected on nearly everything. You were there for me when most people weren't. Your mental health background and education have additionally been a plus to have in our friendship. I want to thank you for all the texts and calls to my mom while I was in the unit, keeping her sane. Without you, I'm sure life would have been hell for her back home. Thank you for calling me while I was there, too. We did everything together. We were that duo that got told we looked like sisters regularly, talked similarly, and eventually intertwined our families. Making us that much closer as we grew closer to each other's siblings and parents. We ruled our little worlds at one point. I'll never forget not only how it felt living with my person but also to have her room three feet away. The amount of memories we made together is something no one can take away. I'll forever cherish those memories. I will forever be grateful for our friendship and the things you taught me about life. I miss and love you dearly. I always will. I wish you nothing but the best and hope time is gracious to us. Thank you, my person, in another life.

Finally, thank you:

To all the people who taught me lifelong lessons, thank you so much.

To all the people who hurt me, thank you for your tests.

To all the people who left, thank you for instilling independence into me,

To all the boys I loved before, thank you for the lessons. You've made me stronger and more confident.

To anyone who's done me wrong, thank you for creating the strong woman I am today. I forgive you.

To anyone who has shown me support throughout my journey, thank you.

Thank you to God for allowing me yet another chance.

SYNOPSIS

At the age of 23, Karlee is a lost but adventurous young adult who sets out on her most avoided but needed journey yet—learning self-love and care toward herself. She does this by entering a behavioral unit for the very first time.

By documenting her stay through journal-like entries that show both the positive and difficulty of in-patient mental health treatment, Karlee provides readers the opportunity to understand mental health through the eyes of a patient and warrior undergoing treatment.

"That's the thing about being here. There's no judgment, and everyone understands depression and anxiety.

Everyone understands, no matter what mental health issue you have. There's no need to explain. There are no looks of pity or judgment."

ABOUT THE AUTHOR

Karlee Jo Mertens is an up-and-coming author who was born and raised in a small town of 3,000 in South Dakota. Growing up on a farm with cattle, show pigs, dogs, and cats, she was raised with a "never give up" attitude by her parents. Karlee Jo's parents also instilled faith, love, and hope into not only herself but also her two sisters, whom she loves dearly.

Her love of writing created Grippy Sock Vacation, a book based on journal entries from her time in a behavioral hospital at the age of 23 and her journey afterward.

After struggling for years with mental health struggles, she now advocates for removing the stigma that impacts so many and stops them from seeking help, including in-patient treatment. To hear more from Karlee and see how she's doing or to listen to words of encouragement, affirmations, or coping skills, visit her website at www.unwellwarriors.com.

CITATIONS

Rnic, K., Dozois, D. J. A., and Martin, R. A. (2016, August 19). *Cognitive distortions, humor styles, and Depression.* Europe's journal of psychology.

https://www.ncbi.nlm.nih.gov/pmc/articles/PMC499104
4/#:~:text=These%20include%20mindreading%20(i.e.

%2C%20assuming,spectrum%20and%20range%20of%
20possible